7, 37

HOW TO USE
THE
LAWS OF MIND

BY

Joseph Murphy, D.D., Ph.D., LL.D., D.R.S.

DeVorss & Company, Publishers
P.O. Box 550
Marina del Rey, California 90291

ISBN: 0-87516-426-9
Library of Congress Card Catalog Number:
80–68548

Printed in the United States of America
by Book Graphics, Inc., Marina del Rey, California

HOW TO USE
THE
LAWS OF MIND

CONTENTS

by Fears and Guilt—The Two Selves in You—The
Road to Success

How She Experienced an Illumination—The Holy of
Holies—The Prayer of Faith—How She Prayed for
Her Brother-in-Law—The Promises of God—You
Are a Mediator—Angels Watch Over You—Are You
Omnipresent?—Nearer to Thee—Is It Wise?—The
Patron Saint—You Can Build a Glorious Future—
You Are the Captain on the Bridge—Age Is Not the
Flight of Years—He's a Medical Marvel—Her Reli-
gion Was Her Problem

You Can Rise—Begin to Believe—The Meaning of
the Blood of the Lamb—The Price You Pay—Why
He Was Disappointed—How He Conquered Despondency—The Prince of this World—How to Handle Fear—There Is an Easier Way—The Secrets of
Life—The Answer to Doom and Gloom—They
Called Him the Rock of Gibraltar—Don't Compare
Yourself with Others—He Wanted to Become a Minister—Law of Cause and Effect—A Better Future

—They Were Paralyzed for 16 Years—Self-Healing—
Expectant Attention—The Value of Laughter—Hyp-
ertension—She Cured Her Jealousy—She Stopped
Stealing from Herself—The Trouble Was Within
Himself—Look Within Always for the Cause—You
Can Call on Your Reserves—The Doctor Said She
Was "Accident Prone"

How Your Mind Works—Changing Your Name—
What Do You Believe?—Born to Win—The Seven
Seals—Who Are You?—Discover Yourself—Lake of
Fire

Finding Your True Place—Her Special Prayer—
Claim Your Good Now—The Present Moment—He
Stopped Blaming Providence—One Life Principle—
Why She Failed to Prosper—Divine Discontent

The Eye Was Called the Devil—God Upside-Down—
Man's Invention—Pain Is a Consequence—Conquering Obstacles—The Fall of Lucifer—One Creative

Power—Truth Sets You Free—Archangel Lucifer—Hebrew Symbolism Referring to the So-Called Devil—Thought Is Creative—There Is No Death—Life Seeks Expression—The Physical Death of the Body—Positive and Negative—The Accuser—Satan—Live and Evil—Casting Out Devils—Auto-Suggestion

Face Your Fears—The Secret Place—Bible Techniques—A Bible Verse Saved Her Estate—Who Is Your Lord?—Guilt and What It Means—Use Your Imagination—God Is Timeless and Spaceless—God and Good Are Synonymous—Prayer Casts Out Fear—Let Divine Love Go Before You

How Suggestion Works—Your Auto-Suggestion—The Wonders of Your Deeper Mind—She Visited a Kahuna—Healers—The Fetish Worshipper—North American Indian Healings—Truth Is Eternal—Overcoming Alcoholism—Darwin's Comments—Control of Animals—She Had a Remarkable Recovery—Paralytics Walk and Run—The Annals of Medicine—Husband Has Morning Sickness

CHAPTER 1

How Your Mind Works

You have only one mind, but there are two phases or functions of that mind. In this chapter I plan to make the distinctions clear and readily comprehensible. Each phase is characterized by its own phenomenon, which is peculiar to itself. Each of these minds is capable of independent action, but that still does not mean that you are endowed with two minds.

In this book you will learn to use both phases of your mind synchronously, harmoniously and peacefully, thereby bringing harmony, health and abundance into your life. The terms used to designate these two functions of your mind are as follows: the "objective mind" and the "subjective mind," the "conscious" and the "subconscious mind." Others designate the two states of consciousness as the "supraliminal" and the "subliminal," after the old psychologists.

I have adopted the terms "conscious" and "subconscious" throughout this book. The objective, or conscious, mind takes cognizance of the objective world by means of the five objective senses, whereas the subconscious, or subjective, mind is that intelligence

1

which manifests itself in all subjective states and conditions, as in dreams, visions of the night, solutions to problems, the source of inspiration, guidance, healing, etc. Your subconscious mind is the mind that takes care of all your vital organs when you are sound asleep. It takes charge of your breathing, the circulation of your blood, and sees to it that your heart and all the other essential functions of your body are operating perfectly. Your conscious mind is your guide in your contact with the environment. You are constantly learning through your five senses by observation, experience and education.

Suggestions and Your Subconscious

Your subconscious mind is amenable to suggestions and it is controlled by suggestion. One of the corollaries of the law of suggestion is that your subconscious mind does not engage in inductive reasoning, which means that it does not institute a line of research by collecting facts, classifying them and estimating their relative evidential values.

Its method of reasoning is purely deductive. This is true whether the premise is true or false. In other words, its deductions from a false premise are as logically correct as from a true one. Thus, if it is suggested to a hypnotized subject that he is a dog, he will immediately play that role and perform the acts of a dog, so far as it is physically possible to do so, while at the same time believing himself to be a dog.

In all probability, you have seen hypnotized subjects

play the role of the type of character suggested to them by the operator or hypnotist, for the subject believes himself to be the actual personality suggested. For instance, you could suggest to a hypnotized subject that he is President Roosevelt; and if at some time in the past he had heard President Roosevelt speak or address the nation, his own personality would be completely submerged under the influence of the suggestion. He would believe himself to be the late President Roosevelt.

Two Opposing Suggestions

You have the power to reject the suggestions of the other person. The suggestions of the other person have no power unless you accept them; then they become the movement of your own mind, or an auto-suggestion. For example, if you say to a businessman or a professional man who is full of confidence and faith in his ability and understanding and who believes in success and achievement that he is going to fail, he laughs at you or treats the suggestion with scorn or ridicule. Actually, your suggestion acted as a stimulus to his conviction of advancement, prosperity and a triumphant life. Your subconscious accepts the dominant of two ideas.

How She Handled the Suggestion of Seasickness

On one of our Seminars on the Sea, a woman suggested to a member of our group that she looked ill and pale and that perhaps the rough sea was making her ill. She was prepared, however. She knew how to handle it, so her rejoinder was: "I am here to have a wonderful time. I am going to roll with the waves and the rhythm of the deep. It is wonderful!" She neutralized the woman's negative suggestion.

The negative suggestions of others, to be effective, must have a kindred spirit in you; a fear pattern must be in your subconscious; otherwise, it would have no effect. Always remember that you can tune in with the Infinite Presence and Power within you. When you are aligned with the Infinite, you will gradually build up an immunity to all harm and false suggestions.

Your Early Training

All of us, when we were young, malleable and highly impressionable, received suggestions regarding religious beliefs, opinions, superstitions, false beliefs and prejudices from our parents, uncles, aunts, clergymen, teachers and others.

All of us accepted the suggestions, beliefs, language, customs and traditions of our parents and environment. We had no other choice. We could not reject their suggestions and indoctrination, as we had not yet reached the point in our lives of discernment or the capacity to differentiate between that which is false and that which is true.

You were not born with any religious beliefs, fears, taboos or strictures of any kind. Like all of us, you were born helpless, ignorant and completely at the

4

mercy of your parents or those entrusted with your care. You were born with only two fears—the fear of falling and the fear of noise—both of which represent God's alarm system in you to protect you. All other fears were given to you.

I suggest to people that they examine the origin of their beliefs, religious concepts, and fears and see if they contribute to their health, happiness and peace of mind. You can eradicate and expunge from your subconscious mind anything that was learned, acquired or copied by you in your youth. In other words, you can recondition or reprogram your subconscious mind along the lines of eternal verities, which are universal and belong to all men. These eternal truths are the same yesterday, today and forever.

How She Cleansed Her Mind

An elderly woman, a retired school teacher, explained to me how she had eradicated what she called her weird, grotesque, irrational, illogical and unscientific religious beliefs. She read a statement from one of the magazines, wherein Einstein said: "Science without religion is lame and religion without science is blind."

She studied the religions of the world, including Unity and Religious Science, and read *The Power of Your Subconscious Mind.** The latter book stopped

---

*See "The Power of Your Subconscious Mind" by Dr. Joseph Murphy. Prentice-Hall, Inc., Englewood Cliffs. N.J.. 1963.

5

her in her tracks. She said it rang a bell and she woke up from a long religious stupor.

Accordingly, she practiced the following prayer regularly and systematically, knowing that she would erase all false concepts of God from her deeper mind in the same way as you talk over a tape, automatically erasing the contents. The reconditioning of her subconscious mind was as follows:

"Divine love fills my soul. Divine right action is mine. Divine harmony governs my life. Divine peace fills my soul. Divine beauty is mine. Divine joy fills my soul. I am Divinely guided in all ways. I am illumined from On High. I know and believe that God's will for me is a greater measure of life, love, truth and beauty, something transcending my fondest dreams. I know that God loves me and cares for me."

She formulated the above prayer after reading *The Power of Your Subconscious Mind* and other books. She knew that by reiterating these great truths, they would sink gradually into her subconscious mind and bring about a transformation.

The first thing she learned was that there is only One Power. There cannot be two, spiritually, scientifically, mathematically or any other way. There is no room for anything else when you realize that God is the Living Spirit Almighty and is omnipresent and omnipotent. If there were two powers, one would cancel out the other and there would be no order, design, proportion or symmetry. The world would be a chaos instead of a cosmos.

She also realized that all the good and evil she experienced were due to the way she used the One Power, which is whole and perfect in Itself. She woke up to the fact that she could use any power two ways and that good and evil were the movements of her own mind relative to the One Being, which is whole and perfect in Itself.

She was a wise woman. She learned from her mistakes and corrected them, instituting new action upon the basis of new truths she has learned. She is now leading a happier and more peaceful experience.

How Can I Find Peace?

This was a question asked me recently at a club in Leisure World. A woman asked: "How can I find peace? I read about rapes, murders, burglaries, gas shortages, and all the crooked deals in high places." My answer to her was that changed attitudes change everything. I pointed out to her that single-handedly she could not change the world or prevent social upheavals, crime and man's inhumanity to man, but she could tune in with the Infinite Presence frequently and affirm: "God's peace fills my soul. The light of God shines in me. I think, speak and act from the Divine Center within me."

This, I added, is the one sure method to find peace in this changing world. There is no law that compels you to hate, resent or fear simply because of what politicians, circumstances or newspapers suggest. You can affirm: "God thinks, speaks and acts through me."

7

HOW TO USE THE LAWS OF MIND

Remember a simple truth of life: No man, circumstance, condition or broadcast takes your peace; you give it away by surrendering your own control over your thoughts, words, deeds and reactions. You are the boss; you are in charge of your own thoughts.

Wealth Was in His Mind

Some weeks ago, I spent some time giving a series of lectures in the major cities of The Republic of South Africa. Dr. Reg Barrett lectures all over the Republic on the laws of mind, and he introduced me at the various seminars we conducted.

After one of the lectures in Durban, a man chatted with me, saying: "You know, it is true. Wealth is first in the mind and then in the ground, the air, the sea, and everywhere." He pointed out that his father and grandfather had come from England to seek their fortunes in South Africa. His grandfather spent many months searching for gold and found nothing. He gave up, because he had no more money. His father, on the other hand, went over the same territory and in a few weeks found a gold vein which subsequently became one of the many famous gold mines in South Africa.

He said that his father was a very religious man and he constantly prayed that God would reveal to him where the gold was and lead him to green pastures and still waters. It is true the gold was in the earth, but the mental and spiritual wealth was in the mind of his father in the form of an implicit belief in Divine guidance and the truths of the 23rd Psalm. Apparently, from what I was told, his grandfather was tense, anxious and jealous because some of his friends had struck it rich and he hadn't. This attitude caused a mental and spiritual blindness, so he could not see the gold under his feet.

Look Within

Do not look outside yourself for peace of mind, wealth, security or inner strength. The Divine Presence is within you—the Supreme Intelligence which created all things and is All-Wise. No government, institution or person can bestow on you the quiet mind or inner peace.

Your subconscious mind is the seat of habit, and habits are built up in the same way you learned to walk, swim, dance, play the piano, type or drive a car. You repeated certain thought patterns and actions over and over, and after a certain length of time these patterns were implanted in your subconscious mind. Now you do these things automatically. You might call this second nature. The latter is simply the response of your deeper mind to your conscious choices and actions.

Frequently during the day, affirm: "God's river of peace saturates my mind and heart. I rest in the everlasting arms of wisdom, truth and beauty." Make a habit of repeating this prayer. Repeat it over and over again, knowing what you are doing and why you are doing it. As you continue to affirm and reiterate these simple truths, you will become peaceful and harmonious, and you will contribute to the peace and serenity of all those around you.

Many say to me that they would love to find some hamlet, some town near the beaches, where they could find rest and comfort. Remember, you take your mind with you wherever you go. Actually, you meet yourself at all times. If the mind is in turmoil and you are anxious and worried, the beach or the mountain will not give you peace. You must *choose* peace.

Some people are unceasingly searching for a Shangri-La where all is bliss and harmony, a sort of Utopia, where all of us will share everything together and live harmoniously, peacefully and joyfully. You must remember, however, that you create your own Utopia. There is no such place except in the mind of man, who is in tune with the Infinite and who has found the peace that passeth understanding. The problems, challenges, difficulties and turmoil around us incite us to find that inner peace and also enable us to discover our Divinity and rise above the problems of the world.

You Can Change Yourself

Remember, you do not have a mystic wand enabling you to change the world, but you can change yourself by identifying yourself with the Infinite Presence and

Power within you and constantly claiming harmony, peace, beauty, love, joy, right action and Divine law and order. As you make a habit of this, you will rise above the turbulence and chaos of the world mind, sometimes referred to as the race mind, law of averages, or mass mind.

Overcome the World

The world, in Biblical language, represents all the people in the world, some good, some bad. The mass mind, or law of averages, means the way four and a half billion people are thinking. Every day you read of wars, cruelty, crime, hate, jealousy, murder, race conflicts and religious struggles. You also read of the good and noble people who contribute to the peace of the world.

You cannot run away from the world or the mass mind. All of us are immersed in it because, subjectively, we are all one and the psychic sea impinges on all of us. That is why you should keep prayed up. Assume now, today, that Infinite Intelligence is guiding and directing you and that the power of the Infinite animates and sustains you. Radiate love, peace, and goodwill to all people and wish for them all the blessings of life.

This attitude will guarantee you success along all lines. Furthermore, you will be contributing to the welfare of all people everywhere. You can definitely move triumphantly through the maelstrom of this confused world into ways of pleasantness and paths of peace. Your inner assumptions, beliefs and convictions dictate and control all external actions.

You Can Transcend

A male nurse—a recent graduate—got a responsible position in a nearby medical clinic. He came to me for consultation, saying that his nerves were jangled, the patients were half crazy, the phones were ringing all the time, and that he couldn't take it any longer.

During the course of our conversation, it began to dawn on him that the people waiting in the clinic were sick mentally as well as physically and that, being a nurse, his job was to overcome the noise, confusion and complaints in that institution. I said to him that the irritations of the sick were a basic part of his work, that he must rise above these problems, and that if he were to run away, he would be going from the frying pan into the fire. I reiterated that he must meet his problems head on and grapple with them courageously; then he would overcome.

He listened, and at my suggestion began to affirm: ". . . *None of these things move me. . .* (Acts 20:24). I will overcome all vexations and difficulties." He decided to remain in the clinic and discovered that his new attitude changed everything.

How He Changed His Life

I had an interesting conversation with a man in Johannesburg, who told me that at 45 years of age he was broke, dispirited, depressed and dejected because his business had failed and his wife had left him because she felt that he could not support her in the way to which she was accustomed.

The turning point in his life, however, came one evening when he attended a lecture on the laws of mind. The first thing the speaker had said was, "Man is what he thinks all day long." This made a profound impression upon him. The speaker added that this truth has been known for thousands of years, but that the rank and file of humanity overlook it or pay little or no attention to it.

For as he thinketh in his heart, so is he. . . (Proverbs 23:7). The heart is an old term for your subconscious mind. All the Bible is saying is that whatever you really think and feel to be true deep down in your heart will come forth and be expressed in all phases of your life. In other words, any thought, idea or concept emotionalized and felt as true will be brought forth by your subconscious as form, function, experience and event. All through the ages this has been the most outstanding discovery in man's life.

This man began to make a habit of thinking of success, harmony, peace, goodwill, prosperity and right action. He busied his mind with these concepts and proceeded to prove them to himself. When thoughts of self-condemnation or self-criticism came to his mind, he said that he would immediately affirm: "Success is mine. Harmony is mine. Abundance is mine." After some months of this altered mental attitude, he became a constructive thinker. He said he now has a business bringing him an income of over several million dollars a year in our money. He employs hundreds of people and shares his profits with them.

The Psalmist said: . . . *I will set him on high, because he hath known my name* (Psalms 91:14). Name means nature, and the nature of Infinite Intelligence is to respond to you. In the third chapter of Exodus, the name is called I AM, or awareness, the function of thinking.

Dr. Reginald Barrett, one of the teachers in South Africa, said a very interesting thing to his audience, the essence of which was this: "If you had no mind you could not see me or hear me. You would have no sensation of the world around you. You could not taste, feel, or smell the fragrance of the flowers in your garden." Your mind is basic to all living, and it gives life, substance and form to what you accept and believe to be true. Everything you look at came out of the invisible mind of man and of God.

Be Sure to Remember a Basic Truth

William James, the father of American psychology, stated that he felt the greatest discovery of the last one hundred years was the awareness of the powers of the subconscious mind. Dr. Phineas Quimby, who started healing people in 1847, pointed out in his experiments that, "If I really believed a thing, the effect would follow whether I was thinking of it or not."

HOW YOUR MIND WORKS

This is of great importance, because it applies to all of us and reveals that whatever has been deposited in our subconscious mind governs and controls us. In other words, your subconscious beliefs, assumptions and convictions dictate, control and direct all your conscious actions, whether you are thinking about them or not. Whatever is impressed in your subconscious mind, whether good or bad, will always be expressed on the screen of space. Your habitual thinking is gradually absorbed and recorded in your subconscious. There they become laws and beliefs which act automatically.

She Was Allergic to Orange Juice

I had a long talk in Port Elizabeth with a young woman who said that she loved to drink orange juice, but that whenever she did, she would break out in a very disagreeable and irritating rash on her face and arms. Her sister and brother, however, drank orange juice with impunity and seemed to thrive on it.

I explained to her that her allergic response undoubtedly went back to childhood, when she ate too many oranges and was told they are bad for her. I pointed out that that belief is now buried in her subconscious mind and predisposes her to a certain reaction, and that the absence of this belief in her brother and sister prevents a similar reaction. It was the subconscious assumption behind the allergic reaction which she had long forgotten.

I explained how she could overcome the problem by using the following prayer, which would recondition her subconscious and erase the fear of oranges: "God pronounced everything good. Whatever I eat or drink is transmuted into beauty, order, symmetry and proportion. I am harmonized and vitalized. I eat the bread of heaven and I drink the wine of joy. In my body I see order, peace, wholeness and beauty made manifest. It is wonderful!"

She was to write these truths by repetition into her subconscious mind so that gradually she would be freed from the false belief. She knew that the conscious mind controls the subconscious, and a few days ago I received a letter from her containing a picture of her drinking orange juice. Having discovered the power within herself, she has found a new sense of freedom and peace of mind.

Practice This Truth

Anything that your conscious mind assumes to be true is accepted by your subconscious mind, and the Infinite Intelligence of your subconscious proceeds to bring to pass and execute the role suggested by your assumption. Your assumption, true or false, hardens into fact and is projected on the screen of space.

He Said, "It Works"

A few months ago, I said in one of my Sunday morning lectures at the Saddleback Theatre in El Toro

16

that whatever a person added to "I AM" with feeling and understanding would come to pass. One man said to himself, "I am going to try it." Accordingly, many times a day he would affirm, out loud when possible, "I AM prosperous. I AM healthy. I AM happy. I feel wonderful!" Driving along the road his silent speech was the same. He made a habit of it and found it to be a valid law of life. His business, his health and his relationship with his family have undergone a marked transformation. He discovered that his changed attitude changed everything in his life.

Your Right Hand

Recently a man gave me a news article in which it stated that a man's hand was cut off at the wrist because he had stolen twice. The article said it was based on the Koran. All Bibles of the world have an inner meaning and should not be taken literally. In Matthew 5:30, it says: *And if thy right hand offend thee, cut it off, and cast it from thee. . . .*

The Bible is full of parables, allegories, metaphors, similes and cryptic statements. A parable has an outer as well as an inner meaning. With the hand, you fashion, mold, create and direct. The action of your hand is, of course, dictated by your thoughts. If, for example, you paint a monstrous, ugly picture, you can change your mind by identifying yourself with the indescribable beauty of God and paint a thing of beauty and a joy forever.

HOW TO USE THE LAWS OF MIND

If your work or your artistic creations are wholly unproductive, stop the endeavor at once and cut it out. In other words, change your mental attitude. If you are not getting results in business or your profession, this is due to your thought life and your imagery. You must change your thoughts.

In one of the Eastern countries, I asked the guide the meaning of the sign in the park. He said that literally it means, "Cut off your feet," which, in our language, means, "Keep off the grass." . . . *Without a parable spake he not unto them* (Matthew 13:34).

And if thy right eye offend thee, pluck it out, and cast it from thee. . . (Matthew 5:29). Eye means spiritual perception, your understanding, the way you look at things, your outlook on life. When a boy understands a complicated algebraic equation, he says, "I see it now," meaning he comprehends it thoroughly.

If you say that there is no way out or you will never get ahead in life, you should pluck out that eye. In other words, cut out that stupid attitude and realize you are a son of the Infinite, born to win. Realize that you are Divinely guided and live in the joyous expectancy of the best, and the best will come to you. Begin to see tongues in trees, sermons in stones, songs in running brooks, and God in everything.

CHAPTER 2

How Your Mind Heals You

Any form of belief which inspires the faith of the patient, when supplemented by a corresponding palliative suggestion, is efficacious as a therapeutic agency. Thus, the fetish worshipper who believes that the tooth or claw of an animal or a carving in wood or bone is the abode of a supernatural spirit, whose aid can be invoked by certain ceremonies, may, by the performance of the prescribed rites, be restored to perfect health. Why? Simply because the ceremony and belief constitute a powerful suggestion, and his subconscious mind and blind faith resurrect and activate the infinite healing presence in his subconscious mind.

The Days of Primitive Humanity

In the days of primitive humanity, when superstition was universal, there prevailed innumerable techniques and methods for the healing of mind and body. The irrational reverence for idols, talismans, bones of saints, relics, etc., brought about healings due to blind faith. The latter means anything that moves your mind from fear to faith, which produces results.

HOW TO USE THE LAWS OF MIND

The Power of the Placebo

A placebo is a medicine or preparation, an inactive one, such as a lactose tablet, or bread crumb in capsule or pill form prepared to soothe a patient. The substance given has no therapeutic value, yet frequently a remarkable healing follows the administration of such innocuous substances. Many doctors in many parts of the world are very much aware of the therapeutic potency of a placebo.

The word placebo is derived from Latin and means "to please." Recently, I read an article which pointed out that Dr. Shapiro stated in the *American Journal of Psychotherapy* that a "placebo can have profound effects on organic illnesses, including incurable malignancies."

Centro Medico Del Mar Tijuana

I have talked with several men and women who told me that they had had cancer, some of the cases being inoperable. They went to the medical clinic in Tijuana, Mexico, received Laetrile treatment, and recovered completely. One man told me that he met people there from all parts of the world. Many articles have appeared in our newspapers about people who were healed by Laetrile when everything else failed.

This points out clearly the working of the subconscious mind, which responds according to the belief of the patient. The Food and Drug Administration and

20

many of the leading cancer specialists state that Laetrile, which is derived from apricots, has no therapeutic value whatsoever. Granting that Laetrile has no medicinal value whatever, if the patient takes it and believes he is going to get well, his belief alters his body chemistry and mobilizes the healing powers of his subconscious mind. . . . *As thou hast believed, so be it done unto thee. . .* (Matthew 8:13).

The Laying On of Hands

The healing of the sick by touch and by the laying on of hands is a very ancient method of healing and is to be found among the earliest nations—among the Indians, the Egyptians and the Jews. In Egypt, sculptures have been found where one hand is represented on the stomach and the other on the back. The Chinese, according to the early missionaries, healed various ailments by the laying on of hands.

In the Old and the New Testaments we find numerous examples, of which a few are selected:

And the Lord said unto Moses, Take thee Joshua the son of Nun, a man in whom is the spirit, and lay thine hand upon him. . . . And thou shalt put some of thine honour upon him, that all the congregation of the children of Israel may be obedient (Numbers 27:18, 20).

. . . They shall lay hands on the sick, and they shall recover (Mark 16:18).

And it came to pass, that the father of Publius lay

21

sick of a fever and of a bloody flux: to whom Paul entered in, and prayed, and laid his hands on him, and healed him (Acts 28:8).

And Ananias went his way, and entered into the house; and putting his hands on him said, Brother Saul, the Lord, even Jesus, that appeared unto thee in the way as thou camest, hath sent me, that thou mightest receive thy sight, and be filled with the Holy Ghost. And immediately there fell from his eyes as it had been scales: and he received sight. . . (Acts 9:17–18).

And they bring unto him one that was deaf, and had an impediment in his speech; and they beseech him to put his hand upon him. And he took him aside from the multitude, and put his fingers into his ears, and he spit, and touched his tongue; And looking up to heaven, he sighed, and saith unto him, Eph-pha-tha, that is, Be opened. And straightway his ears were opened, and the string of his tongue was loosed, and he spake plain (Mark 7:32–35).

There are many other passages in the Bible, all of which testify to the wonderful therapeutic efficacy of the laying on of hands. We are told in the Bible that when Jesus visited his native village, he did not do many mighty works there because of their unbelief. But the Bible writer, in relating the circumstance, adds this significant statement: *And he could there do no mighty work, save that he laid his hands upon a few sick folk, and healed them* (Mark 6:5).

It is said that St. Patrick, the Irish apostle, healed the blind by laying his hands upon them. History tells us that the Kings of England and France cured diseases by touch. It is said that the pious Edward the Confessor and Philip the First of France were the first kings who possessed this power. The laying on of the hands was called chirothesia.

Many healers all over the world today practice the laying on of hands, and many get wonderful results. Many claim that there is a magnetic healing power flowing through their hands which is transmitted to every cell. It is reasonable to assume that the belief of the practitioner and the receptivity, faith and kindled imagination on the part of the patient bring about an impregnation of the subconscious mind, thereby releasing and activating the infinite healing presence.

The Bible gives the answer: . . . *According to your faith be it unto you* (Matthew 9:29).

The Power of Belief

I had a phone call from a woman in Utah, with whom I had been in correspondence. She was suffering from terminal cancer and was praying for guidance, wholeness and perfection. She had been saying, "I don't want an operation. I don't want to go to the hospital. I don't want to see a surgeon."

I explained to her that she should never make any such statements, as they indicate fear and cause her to experience the very thing she is afraid of: *For the thing*

23

which I greatly feared is come upon me . . . (Job 3:25). Furthermore, I explained to her that it was wrong for her to dictate the way the healing would come, as the ways of the Infinite Presence are past finding out. She kept on praying for guidance, wholeness, beauty and perfection.

A friend told her about a book published by Dr. John Richardson and Patricia Griffin, describing 90 cases of cancer sufferers who were healed by treatment with Laetrile. She went down to Tijuana, took the treatment, kept on praying and had a full recovery. She went there believing and received accordingly.

Therefore I say unto you, What things soever ye desire, when ye pray, believe that ye receive them, and ye shall have them (Mark 11:24). . . . *If thou canst believe, all things are possible to him that believeth* (Mark 9:23).

How Mind Helps Medicine Work

In an article sent to me by Professor Jack Holland of San Jose University, entitled "The Mysterious Placebo," by Norman Cousins, it is stated: "A striking example of the doctor's role in making a placebo work can be seen in an experiment in which patients with bleeding ulcers were divided into two groups. Members of the first group were informed by the doctor that a new drug had just been developed that would undoubtedly produce relief. The second group was told by nurses that a new experimental drug would be

24

administered, but that very little was known about the effect.

Seventy percent of the people in the first group received significant relief from their ulcers. Only twenty-five percent of the patients in the second group experienced similar benefit. Both groups had been given the identical "drug"—a placebo. Norman Cousins makes a very interesting comment when he states that the doctor, himself, is the most powerful placebo of all.

The above-mentioned experiment reveals the power of belief on the part of the patients. One group had great expectancy of a healing on hearing the words from the doctor; the others were not very impressed by the rather weak statement of the nurse regarding the efficacy of the so-called drug and consequently got very poor results. To believe is to accept something as true.

The Father Within

The Father within is the Source of all things and beings. It is the Life-Principle. Jesus called this Presence "Our Father," which created all things visible and invisible. It is the Power which Jesus used to heal the blind, the halt and the lame. It is the mind and intelligence which quiets the storm, which multiplies the loaves and fishes, the mind which enabled Jesus to disappear in the multitude, to converse with Moses and to raise the dead to life.

HOW TO USE THE LAWS OF MIND

When you see a mind like that operating, you know there is the Source and Power called the "Father within." . . . *The Father that dwelleth in me, he doeth the works* (John 14:10). You do not see mind, thought, faith or confidence. The Bible says, . . . *He that hath seen me hath seen the Father* . . . (John 14:9). In other words, if you see a mind performing all these wonderful actions and miraculous healings, you realize that mental and spiritual forces operating are directed by the Father within.

Expect Security

Over the years I have found that a great number of people expect disappointments in life. Many are afraid of some unseen danger; a sense of foreboding, uncertainty and anxiety seems to hover over their mind like a cloud. Great numbers are convinced that the will of God for them is something downright unpleasant and that God is bound to send suffering, difficulties or obstacles of some nature in order to test their faith or punish them for their sins. It is amazing how many people think that the will of God for them is some sort of sickness, pain and punishment for their errors.

Remember, God's will for you is the tendency of the Life-Principle, which always seeks to express Itself as love, beauty, joy, harmony and the life more abundant. The will of God for you is something marvelous, wonderful and beautiful, transcending your fondest

26

dreams. God is absolute peace and cannot wish pain. God is boundless joy and cannot wish sorrow. God is boundless love and cannot do anything unloving. God is wholeness, beauty and perfection and cannot wish sickness. God is the same yesterday, today and forever.

Man brings on suffering, sickness, pain and misery for himself due to his ignorance of the laws of mind and the way of Infinite Spirit. Man must get away from the jungle ideas that God is a personal being with personal feelings of vengeance such as a man may have. God is also universal law, and the law is not vengeful; it is impersonal and no respecter of persons. . . . *God is no respecter of persons* (Acts 10:34).

When man uses the law negatively, he suffers from the reaction of the law. The sun shines on the good and the bad man, on the murderer and the holy man. The rain falls on the just and the unjust, and the Infinite Spirit passes no judgment on any man. Man rewards and punishes himself based on the way his conscious mind impregnates his subconscious mind. If man thinks good, he receives good; and if he thinks evil, evil inevitably follows. It is as simple as that.

. . . *How can ye, being evil, speak good . . . ?* (Matthew 12:34). Rewards and punishments are inherent in man's own thinking and imagery. It is very foolish for him to postulate the cause of his good fortune or misfortune outside himself.

27

He Discovered Himself

Recently a man came to me for consultation. He was working for a large corporation and he was blaming his associates, the boss and the corporation. He imagined certain people in the office were blocking his promotion and advancement. He was angry about these conditions and circumstances, which caused quarrels and disharmony of all sorts.

I explained to him that the cause of all his experiences was in himself, not outside, and that he had wandered away from his Divine Center, the Source and Cause of all blessings. This man was as though blindfolded and fighting enemies that were not really there. He changed his attitude and began to claim morning and night the following: "God is on my side. God loves me and cares for me. God is my boss, my guide, and opens up the way for greater expression for me." He decided to change his thought life and began to radiate thoughts of love and goodwill to all his associates, the boss and all others around him.

He discovered that God, the Supreme Intelligence within him, was for him and not against him. To think otherwise would be a complete contradiction in purpose and motivation. He discovered that the so-called enemies were but a projection of his own fears and ignorance. His changed attitude changed everything.

There is an old saying: "Peace is the power at the heart of God." This man came to peace within himself and he began to project this inner peace on all people and conditions. Peace is at the center of our being and is the soul of the universe. Because he was now in agreement with his Divine Center, he found his way to advancement and true expression.

He Said, "I Did Not Believe It About Myself"

A few years ago after speaking in Caxton Hall, London, a man invited me to have tea with him. He brought up a very interesting subject about publicity. Some years previously he had hired a publicity man to promote him politically and project the ideal image. He said that he was elected to the office three times but that he felt he had deceived his people, as he was not the man which the publicity writer had stated he was.

He said he knew what they were doing, as he knew the law of mind: They were making repetitive suggestions in various newspapers and on the radio and television, and, apparently, the people had accepted and believed what they had heard so often. He related that "in my heart I did not feel right about it, as I had nothing but contempt for the people. I looked down upon them as ignorant, boorish and gullible." He said that the artificially projected image of himself was completely false, as he did not have anything like that self-image himself.

This man had a great conflict in his mind and had developed bleeding ulcers. A psychosomatic doctor in

London explained the cause of his condition to him. He had a guilt complex and felt he should be punished because he was deceiving the public and claiming certain virtues and characteristics which he did not possess. The medicine and the subsequent retirement from politics had healed his ulcers.

I explained to him that it was essential to have a good self-image. He decided to affirm boldly: "I am a son of the Living God. God loves me and cares for me. I exalt God in the midst of me. God is, and His Presence flows through me as harmony, health, peace, joy and abundance." I suggested that he make this simple prayer a habit by frequent repetition, and whenever he is prone to criticize or find fault with himself, he is to immediately affirm: "I exalt God in the midst of me."

I also explained to him that when he looks down on others, belittling and demeaning them, he is doing the same thing to himself for the simple reason that he is the only thinker, and whatever he thinks he is creating in his body and experience. This man discovered God within himself and is no longer down on himself.

Don't Fight the World

When you open your newspaper in the morning or listen to the evening news on radio or television, you may read or hear about shocking cruelties and tragedies in the world. If you resent all the crime, rape and murders or try to fight these things in your mind, getting angry and upset, you will always be at odds, and, being inharmonious within, you will manifest disharmony in all phases of your life.

Realize that God's peace fills your soul and that God's love saturates your mind and heart. Furthermore, claim, feel and know that the light of God shines in all humanity. You are then contributing, to some degree, to peace in this changing world. Cease wasting your precious mental and spiritual energy in fighting and opposing worldly conditions. Use your energy constructively and create health and happiness for yourself and all those around you.

Remember Not the Former Things

I talked briefly with a man in a local club to which I belong, who is over 80 years of age. He enumerated all the grievances he had against the Social Security Administration, the tax situation, how crooked the government was and all the wounds he had received in the two world wars. He spoke of a law suit which had taken place 50 years ago, as well as the money he had lost in the market crash in 1929. He was living with his old hurts and grievances and was full of anger and hate toward the present government in Washington. He carried a cane and was suffering from arthritis and colitis—all brought on by his negative, destructive emotions.

I discussed with him the role of emotions in disease, and he appeared to be receptive. He realized that he could not change the world, but that he could change himself. His mind was traversing old scenes and settings, which generated destructive emotions. I explained to him that these emotions get snarled up in the subconscious and must have an outlet, and, being negative, the result appeared as a sickness in his body.

I suggested that he establish a prayer process, get active in one or two social clubs, make friends, start swimming and take up golf. The pattern of prayer I gave him was to read the 23rd Psalm in the morning, the 27th at noon and the 91st at night prior to sleep. The Psalms are songs of God,* and by saturating his mind with these great truths, he would gradually transform his mind.

The following is the prayer of forgiveness which I gave him: "I claim God's love fills my soul now. I know when His love flows in my heart, all resentment is dissolved. I forgive myself for harboring any negative, destructive thoughts about another. I resolve not to do this any more. I tune in on the Infinite One within me, and I think, speak, act and react from the standpoint of God and His law of love. I fully and freely forgive everyone (mention their names). I radiate love, peace, goodwill and all the blessings of Heaven to them. They are free and I am free. I know when I have released others from my mind because I can meet them in my mind and there is absolutely no 'sting'; on the contrary, there is a wave of peace and a benediction from my heart."

*See *Songs of God. An Interpretation of My Favorite Psalms.* by Dr. Joseph Murphy, DeVorss & Co., Marina del Rey, Ca., 1979.

I see this man occasionally, and he no longer talks of the past but is interested in God and the way He works. The suppleness and mobility of his joints have delighted him and his doctor, and he is on the way to a new life. The cure for his condition was to change his thoughts and keep them changed.

The Two Worlds

When we speak of metaphysics, we refer to that which is above and beyond the physical. It refers to the inner world of your thoughts, feelings, imagination and beliefs. When you stop and think, you realize that everything you do and that you refuse to do is previously determined by an attitude of mind—a way of thinking on your part. If you find your condition chronic, if you are leading a dull, routine, monotonous life, it is very likely that you too are dwelling on the past and repeating the same old mental patterns.

You are here to grow, and when you refuse to let the Life Principle move through you at higher levels, It has no alternative but to, perhaps, bring about some negative experience such as sickness or other problems, which will arouse you out of your lethargy and cause you to find the solution. In that way, you discover yourself.

Peace of Mind

The Bible says, . . . *I came not to send peace, but a sword* (Matthew 10:34). Jesus is called the Prince of

Peace. Obviously, you must look for the deep psychological and spiritual meaning behind the words. The Bible is stating an age-old truth, referring to the Divine wisdom in every man. When you hear the real truth about yourself for the first time and learn that you mold, fashion and create your own destiny, you are disturbed, perhaps shocked, and your mind is divided.

Symbolically, a sword severs, cuts clean. You are dealing here with the sword of division, which separates the false concepts from the truth.

One Sunday morning after one of my lectures on The Power of Your Subconscious Mind,* one girl said she was shocked out of her religious beliefs, which she had had since childhood. She added that it all rang true; that is why it was so disturbing to her.

I suggested that she begin to identify with the simple truths propounded and practice them to prove to herself that the truth sets her free from outworn creeds, superstitions and theological complexities about a dire hereafter, etc.

Truth, or the sword, comes into your mind in order to separate you from all that is false; therefore, it sets up a quarrel in your mind. Finally, the truth wins and you discover that you are your own savior. If you are sick, health is your savior; if hungry, food is your savior; if in the prison of fear, ignorance and super-

*See *The Power of Your Subconscious Mind* by Dr. Joseph Murphy. Prentice-Hall. Englewood Cliffs. N.J.. 1963.

stition or the prison of stone walls, freedom is your savior; if dying of thirst, water is your savior; and if lost in the jungle, the guiding principle in your subconscious will lead you out provided you call on the Infinite Intelligence residing in your subconscious depths.

The Bible gives the answer: *I, even I, am the Lord; and beside me there is no saviour.* (Isaiah 43:11). *I am the Lord, and there is none else, there is no God beside me: I girded thee, though thou hast not known me* (Isaiah 45:5).

The I AM in you is the Presence of God, Awareness, Pure Being, The Living Spirit, the Creator of all things visible and invisible. This is why every man is his own savior. Truth is saying to you to break away from all beliefs that instill fear into your mind. The peace spoken of is not resignation or putting up with some problem or so-called incurable condition. It means to break away from all such beliefs and absolutely refuse to continue to endure the problem.

Realize that God knows the solution to all problems and go within and boldly claim your good, insisting on harmony, health and an abundant life. Cut yourself away from old, habitual ways of thinking. Reject all predictions of gloom and doom. Expect the highest and the best, and the highest and best will come to you. Learn to walk the earth with the praise of God forever on your lips.

Remember the truths of life are at variance with all

the old thoughts, opinions and religious beliefs you have held, and these truths stir up the gift of God within you. Believe what the Psalmist* says in the 23rd Psalm and you will be led to green pastures and beside the still waters. Find the inner peace that passeth all understanding.

*See *Songs of God: An Interpretation of My Favorite Psalms.* by Dr. Joseph Murphy. DeVorss & Co., Marina del Rey, Ca., 1979.

CHAPTER 3

The Secret of Success in Life

Every person in the world wants to succeed. You are born to win, to conquer and to lead the triumphant life. You should be a wonderful success in your prayer life, your chosen work, your relationship with people and in all other phases of your life.

Success itself is a powerful incentive, for the Life Principle in you is always seeking expression through you at higher levels. You are successful when you lead a full and happy life, when you are expressing yourself at your highest level and contributing your talents to the world. In a successful undertaking you rise as high as you can, and your enterprise is of benefit to humanity. It brings you material reward and its production is a pleasure to you. Success is many-sided, however, and what is deemed success by one may be regarded as failure by another.

He Said, "I Am Not a Success"

Recently I talked with a man who said that he had subordinated all ends to money-making, and he had accumulated a vast amount of money and real estate holdings. He added that in the business world he is called a great success. He admitted to me, though, that he was not a success; he had used questionable means to take advantage of others and had won his fortune through cheating and deceiving others who had trusted him. He was presently suffering from bleeding ulcers and extremely high blood pressure. Furthermore, he had a guilt complex, which meant to him that he had to suffer and be punished.

His bleeding ulcer, as I explained to him, was due to ulcerated thoughts. Further, if he would reverse his thought pattern a healing would follow. He was suffering from the side effects of the drugs he was taking. He consequently reversed his thought patterns by reiterating the following truths out loud night and morning:

"The Lord is my shepherd. I sing the song of the jubilant soul for I have chosen God as my shepherd. Divine Intelligence rules and guides me in all my ways. I shall not want for peace, harmony, or guidance because God's wisdom governs me. I lie down in green pastures always, since God is prospering me beyond my wildest dreams. I find myself beside the still waters as I claim the Infinite peace of God floods my mind and heart. My emotions (waters) are stilled and calm. My mind is now serene and it reflects God's heavenly truths and light (my soul is restored). I think of God's Holy Presence within me all day long. I walk the path of righteousness through my devotion and attention to

38

God's eternal verities. I know there is no death and I fear no evil. I know 'God has not given us the spirit of fear, but of love and power, and a sound mind.' God's rod (love) and staff (truth) comfort, sustain and nourish me. The banquet table of God is always set before me; it is the secret place of the Most High, where in my thoughts I walk and talk with God. I eat the nourishing truths of God whenever fear and worry (my enemies) trouble me. The bread I eat is God's idea of peace, love and faith in all things good. The meat I eat is the omnipotence of God; the wine I drink is the essence of joy. The wisdom of God anoints my intellect; it is a lamp unto my feet and a light on my path. My cup (heart) is truly the chamber of God's Holy Presence; it runneth over with love and joy. I mentally dwell on goodness, truth and beauty; this is my house of God."

As he saturated his mind with the interpretation of the 23rd Psalm over a period of time, he noticed a distinct change in his whole demeanor and outlook on life. He became more kindly, considerate and more loving in all ways. Drugs were no longer necessary. He discovered that a changed attitude changed everything.

He ceased condemning himself. The Life Principle never condemns, and when you begin to use your mind in the right way, right results follow. Your mind is a principle, and if you think good, good follows; if you think lack, lack follows. The Life Principle holds no grudges, no more so than the principles of mathematics or chemistry hold grudges.

You may have been fired by companies you worked for because you could not add or subtract correctly, but by following proper instruction you don't make these mistakes any more. The principle of mathematics has no grudge against you. The same is true of your mind. Begin to use the law of mind in the right way according to the Golden Rule and the law of love. The Mind Principle has no grudge against you. The past is forgotten and remembered no more.

The Law of Reversibility

Edison knew that speech produced undulatory waves and theorized that these vibrations could reproduce the speech or song. In other words, he conceived of inverse transformation, the reproduction of speech or song by mechanical motion, namely the phonograph.

Students of scientific laws know that all transformations of force are reversible. Heat produces mechanical motion. Reverse it and you discover that mechanical motion can produce heat. Science says electricity produces magnetism; likewise, magnetism can produce electric currents. Cause and effect, energy and matter, action and reaction are the same and are interconvertible.

Therefore, I say unto you, What things soever ye

desire, when ye pray, believe that ye receive them, and ye shall have them (Mark 11:24). Here you are told to pray, believing that you already possess what you pray for. This is based on the law of inverse transformation.

Achieving Success in Prayer

A mother wished to visit her son in London, who was graduating from college. However, she did not have the necessary funds. I asked her what her attitude would be if she were over there now, embracing him and witnessing the graduation exercises. She said, "Oh! I would be so happy! I would be delighted."

I suggested that she experiment at night prior to sleep, making there here and the future now and to feel herself embracing her son, making the whole scene vivid and realistic—so much so that when she opened her eyes she would be amazed that she was not in London with her son.

Experimenting along these lines, the third night she subjectified the state. When she opened her eyes she was really amazed that she was not physically there. The answer to her prayer came with the repayment of a loan she had given to a woman ten years previously. With the interest added to it, it was more than the amount necessary for her trip.

She assumed that she was already witnessing the ceremony and conversing with her son, and that joyous feeling and assumption brought about the joy of the answered prayer. She contemplated her objective as an accomplished fact. She understood that all transformations of force are reversible. She knew that her physical presence in London would bring her great joy and satisfaction. Capturing in her mind the joy that would be hers in being there, this mood, she knew, must produce the answer to her prayer.

. . . *He . . . calleth those things which be not as though they were* (Romans 4:17). Success in your prayer life is based on laws of mind. Realize that if a physical fact can produce a joyous mental state in you, the joyous mental state can produce the physical fact.

Unscrupulous Methods

When a man uses unscrupulous financial or business methods, he may not suffer financial loss, but loss can come to him in many ways, such as loss of health, loss of promotion, loss of prestige, loss of self respect, loss of love, etc., for the ways of the subconscious are past finding out. All misdeeds or misuse of the law of mind must be accounted for sooner or later.

The only success that permits a man to rest peacefully and harmoniously is that which conforms to the Golden Rule, i.e., to think, speak and act toward others as he would wish others to think, speak, feel and act toward him. Success is primarily moral and spiritual, governed by honesty, integrity and justice and tempered by goodwill to all men everywhere.

All of us are interdependent, and it is reasonable to

assume that the welfare of others is essential to the success of every man. It is undoubtedly true that the more man cares for and appreciates the spiritual life, the more he will use his material wealth wisely, judiciously and constructively.

A spiritually-minded person should be comfortably housed, clothed and fed. In other words, he realizes that all things are here for his use and enjoyment. . . . *God, who giveth us richly all things to enjoy* (I Timothy 6:17).

It is true that no one possesses anything in the absolute sense. God possesses all, but we have the use of God's treasures in the earth, including the sea and the air. A spiritual-minded person should have all the money he needs to do what he wants to do, and when he wants to do it. Money is simply a medium of exchange, and it has taken many forms down through the ages. It is God's way of maintaining the economic health of a nation.

Success in Spiritual Work

You must realize that a spiritual work or a spiritual organization is not a success if it is constantly begging for more money. This practice is evidence of downright failure. This could be called spurious spirituality. If the spiritual approach to life is successful, it is needed by the world and will be supported.

The successful man is not a mere partisan, but a real truth seeker. The spiritual-minded person is not a proselyter, but a co-worker on the way. The secret of the truth seeker is his fidelity to the inner promptings of his Higher Self. The Infinite Presence in each of us grants us the potentialities of success, and we are here to go forth conquering and to conquer.

He Was President of a Large Corporation

Recently I gave some spiritual advice to a president of a very large corporation. He was very successful, had all the money he needed, lived in a million dollar home and had all the comforts and luxuries of life. Of course, there is nothing wrong with that. He came to this country penniless and had reached the top in his field, all of which is good.

However, he was not successful in the art of living. He had very high blood pressure, and suffered from migraine headaches and colitis. He said to me, "I am a nervous wreck. I have tried tranquilizers, sedatives, antispasmodic tablets and nothing seems to help."

I suggested that all he really needed was peace of mind and that no one could give him that but himself. I pointed out to him the direction where he could find it. I suggested that he read and meditate on the inner meaning of the 23rd Psalm* two or three times a day and affirm frequently during the day, "God's peace

*See the meditation on the 23rd Psalm contained in *Within You Is the Power* by Dr. Joseph Murphy. DeVorss and Company. Inc.. Marina del Rey. Ca.. 1977.

fills my soul." I emphasized that if he began to think constructively and about the eternal verities in the 23rd Psalm, he could improve himself physically and find inner peace.

He was desperate and was willing to try anything. I gave him the book *Within You Is the Power,* * in which the inner meaning of the 23rd Psalm is given. He had an open mind and began to meditate on the Psalm and other chapters of the book. He found that inner quietude and peace which he had been seeking. Turning back to the God Presence within and communing with Divine love and Divine peace, his soul was restored.

The Closed and Open Mind

A full cup cannot receive any more. There are some minds so full of false beliefs, opinions, and weird and grotesque concepts of God that it is impossible to insert anything new, vital and constructive. I recently said to an alcoholic, "Admit that you are an alcoholic. Open your mind to new ideas. A closed mind can receive no interpretations of life, no more so than your closed hand can receive a proffered gift of a book from me."

He said that his excessive drinking was all due to pressure and tension at work. He made a great deal of money, but most of it went to the bar. He was hungry and thirsty for a healing. At this point he came to a decision that he wanted to be healed, which in itself is seventy-five per cent of the healing process.

I explained to him that his subconscious mind would accept his whole-souled conviction and that sincerity was essential. At night prior to sleep, he affirmed feelingly, knowingly and lovingly: "God gives me freedom, sobriety and peace of mind. Thank you, Father." That was his prayer for five or six minutes every night. Actually, he was writing with his conscious mind freedom, peace and sobriety in his subconscious mind. In less than a week he succeeded in impregnating his subconscious mind and he lost all desire for alcohol. The law compelled him to freedom, whereas before it compelled him to be a compulsive drinker. You can use any law two ways. He decided to use this one the right way.

The Source of All Blessings

The Bible says: *Come unto me, all ye that labour and are heavy laden, and I will give you rest* (Matthew 11:28). The Bible is a psychological and spiritual textbook and is not referring to a particular man. The characters in the Bible are personifications of truth. You do not go to any person for rest, security or peace of mind. You go to the God of peace within you and boldly claim: "God's river of peace, love and joy is now flowing through me vitalizing, healing and restoring my soul."

THE SECRET OF SUCCESS IN LIFE

The Divine Presence is within you. As you contemplate God's love, light, truth and beauty in your own heart, you are enfranchised and lifted up because you have found God in your own heart. The Divine Center is within you.

The Psalmist says,* *Rest in the Lord, and wait patiently for him...* (Psalm 37:7). The word "Lord" represents spiritually the Lordly power, which is God; but to "rest in the Lord" means to rest and trust that Infinite Spirit in you which created you, governs all your vital organs as you sleep and is in complete control of all externals. In other words, it is your Higher Self.

In ancient times there were feudal barons who had the power of life and death over the serfs, slaves and peasants under their control. The lords in England today represent titled nobility and have no such power. Look at the whole thing this way: The Lord in you is really your dominant conviction, your master thought or belief, which controls and dominates all lesser thoughts, ideas, opinions, actions and reactions. For example, your Lord could be fear, i.e., if you are dominated by fear. If fear predominates, then fear governs and controls all your thoughts, feelings, actions and reactions.

*See *Songs of God. An Interpretation of My Favorite Psalms.* by Dr. Joseph Murphy. DeVorss & Co., Marina del Rey, Ca., 1979.

47

HOW TO USE THE LAWS OF MIND

A wonderful Lord to enthrone in your mind would be a God of love ruling, guiding, and directing you along all lines. This dominant conviction would work wonders in your life, and your whole world would magically melt in the image and likeness of your dominant conviction. When Divine love and Divine right action govern you, the true Lord is ruling in you and will keep you in peace. You will be successful in your work and in your relationships with people. You will have good health and be free from despondency and melancholia.

Your dominant belief rules your world and determines your future, where you shall go and what your experiences will be, whether good or bad. Quimby said in 1847: "Man is belief expressed." You will be assured of success, true expression and harmonious relations with others when you make it a habit to tune in to the Divine Center within you and look upon the Divine Presence within you as your guide, counselor, wayshower and source of your promotion and welfare. Then all the petty, fearful, annoying worries, jealousies and envies will fall away. There is no room for them in your mind any more.

All of us suffer until we get the insight to look within. The Bible says: . . . *In returning and rest shall ye be saved* . . . (Isaiah 30:15).

THE SECRET OF SUCCESS IN LIFE

Successful Living

There is a man of over ninety years, chronologically speaking, who comes to hear me occasionally on Sunday mornings. Recently he said to me that about thirty years ago he had had the same concept of God as he had had when a little boy. His concept was that of an angry, spiteful God, a sort of Oriental sultan who ruled tyrannically. He lived in fear and thought that the will of God was that he should suffer. He became very ill and the doctor said, "You have about two months to live. Get your affairs in order."

A young woman visiting another patient in his hospital room gave him a pamphlet on how to use the Healing Power, which he read avidly. All of a sudden, he had a great thirst and hunger to live. He got up out of bed, insisted on going home, and invited all of his friends to a restaurant for dinner and refreshments. He said, "I am celebrating my resurrection." His belief and new insight into the Infinite Healing Presence within him responded, and this spiritual transfusion transformed his whole life.

He said that he has accomplished far more in the last thirty years than he had in all the previous sixty years. He broke away from all of the old, moth-eaten patterns, the old ruts and false concepts, and entered into a new life wherein he contributed to the success of all those he supervised and befriended.

HOW TO USE THE LAWS OF MIND

Watch Your Words

Your subconscious mind takes you literally. I know a man, a builder, who is about fifty-five years of age. His wife complains that he is constantly saying, "I am getting old. I'm not as strong any more as I used to be. My memory is failing. I can't take it any more." This man looks to be over eighty years old and is experiencing weakness, decrepitude, lack of vitality and the joy of living. She reminds him of the working of his subconscious mind, but he ridicules it and says that there is no such thing as a subconscious mind. His mind is closed and he is expressing what he is impressing on his subconscious mind.

Life never grows old. Age is not the flight of years but the dawn of wisdom. Love, faith, confidence, joy, goodwill, laughter and inspiration never grow old. Life is always seeking expression through you at higher levels whether you are ninety or nine. Learn to listen to the impulses from within. These are the urges of the Spirit, or God, in you, saying to you, "Come on up higher. I have need of you." Welcome the soft tread of the unseen guest in your heart.

. . . I am come that they might have life, and that they might have it more abundantly (John 10:10). This is the urge of the Life Principle within you. It is the Infinite Presence causing you to be aware of the murmurings, whisperings, inspiration and dreams enabling you to move onward, upward and Godward.

50

THE SECRET OF SUCCESS IN LIFE

Triumph of Principles

Emerson said, "Nothing will give you peace but the triumph of principles." You would not wire your house unless you understood and applied the principles of electricity. You would not manufacture chemicals unless you understood the principles of chemistry. In building a house, you must be initiated into the principles of construction. If you decide to become a musician, you must study music and practice, and as time goes on, perhaps you can play a classical piece of music even though blindfolded. You will have established the equivalent in your subconscious mind, which enables you to play automatically.

Your mind is a principle. Think good and good follows; think of lack and limitation and you experience lack and impoverishment. You are what you think all day long. Learn the laws of your mind and practice them. For example, any idea you have which is emotionalized and felt as true enters into your subconscious mind and comes to pass. Knowing that, you are careful how you impress your subconscious mind.

Why They Did Not Pay

During a conversation I had with a practitioner, she mentioned that she gives people a lot of time and good advice but many never pay her. I suggested to her that she could overcome that by affirming that all those who come to her are blessed, healed and prospered and that they gladly pay in Divine order.

She changed her attitude and her subconscious responded. The reason many clients had not paid her was because in the daytime she was a social worker and her subjective thinking was about poor people and poverty. She became very successful following her new insight into the way the mind works.

Some Common Superstitions

Many people say, "If it's the will of God, I want it." If your prayer is preceded by "if," your manifestation will be very "iffy" and probably will never come to pass. A woman seeking companionship said, "I'm too old. I'm homely." She recited all the reasons why she could not get married instead of all the reasons why she could.

I said to the woman who had these defeatist ideas, "The man you are seeking is seeking you. The last time he got married his wife was so beautiful she ran around and slept with all the boys. He does not want that now; he wants you."

I continued by saying that she should read the newspapers and see all the names and ages of people sixty, seventy and eighty years of age getting married. Infinite Spirit will attract to you the right companion in Divine order, but you must claim it. Think of all your good qualities and what you have to give a man. Let that be your broadcast, and by the law of reciprocal relationship, you will attract the right man into your life. Your sincerity will make it real.

She followed these simple instructions and in due course received an answer to her prayer.

Another superstition is, "If it's God's will." That is too absurd for words. The will of God is a greater measure of life, freedom, expression and growth. Any idea or desire that you have for growth, wealth, success or healing is the will of God for you. Focus on your desire. Bring your conscious and subconscious together at one point—then you will bring your desire to pass.

Another superstition is, "If it's right for me." What is not right for you? It is right for you to lead the abundant life. It is right for you to have perfect health, peace, harmony, joy, abundance, security, true place and all the blessings of life. God gave you richly all things to enjoy.

The Law of Mind Is Impersonal

Take a weaver's loom. All threads are on it—black, brown, yellow, etc. The loom takes all the threads and cares not. Supposing you look at a carpet and say that it is awful, an eyesore. Change the thread and the loom is mechanical and responds accordingly. Your conscious mind is the weaver; your subconscious is the loom.

HOW TO USE THE LAWS OF MIND

A man opens up a brothel and makes a lot of money. The subconscious does not care; it has no morals. It expresses what is impressed upon it, whether good or bad. For example, a man may inherit a lot of money. Perhaps he will spend it badly. Perhaps he will gamble and lose it all, or perhaps, if he is of a religious persuasion, he will teach limitation and instill fear into the minds of people.

Remember, the law is impersonal. If you misuse the law by hurting others or by robbing or depriving them in any way, the law of your mind responds in its own way. . . . *Vengeance is mine; I will repay, saith the Lord* (Romans 12:19). Live according to your highest ideals.

A man asked me why it was that sexual perverts and dope fiends write good poetry, music and wonderful plays. The answer is simple: God, or Infinite Intelligence, is no respecter of persons and will respond to the altruist, pervert or murderer, providing he believes; and according to his belief is it done unto him.

Another superstition that some people have is that God is testing them. They have a sort of a Messianic complex that God is up there in the clouds somewhere and is going to drop a great challenge to them to see how they are going to handle it. God does not punish or test anyone. Man punishes himself because of ignorance and misuse of the laws of mind. The only sin is ignorance, and all the suffering in the world is the consequence.

THE SECRET OF SUCCESS IN LIFE

You Are Needed

The poet said: "We are all parts of one stupendous whole whose body nature is and God the soul." There must be joy in your work. In olden days when they made a table, a statue or a chair, there was a song in their heart. They took pride in their work. The larger piece in the table or the building needs the small. All the component parts go to make up the unit. You are needed. There is no misfit in the universe. All notes are necessary for the symphony.

There is no one in all the world who can do something just like you because only you are you. You are unique. If you are a cook you are essential to the General of the army. There is nothing useless but your belief and concept that you are. Your subconscious accepts what you really believe, and you experience accordingly.

Meditation for Success

" 'Wist ye not that I be about my Father's business?'* I know that my business, profession or activity is God's business. God's business is always basically successful. I am growing in wisdom and understanding every day. I know, believe and accept the fact that God's law of abundance is always working for me, through me and all around me.

"My business or profession is full of right action and

*See Luke 2:49.

55

right expression. The ideas, money, merchandise and contacts that I need are mine now and at all times. All these things are irresistibly attracted to me by the law of universal attraction. God is the life of my business; I am Divinely guided and inspired in all ways. Every day I am presented with wonderful opportunities to grow, expand and progress. I am building up goodwill. I am a great success because I do business with others as I would have them do it with me."

CHAPTER 4

The Power of the Spirit:
Saved from the Abyss of Death

Recently I talked with a woman in Munich, Germany, who is 80 years of age, chronologically speaking. She said that her physical condition at one time had been considered hopeless and incurable, but that she had been saved from the abyss of death by spiritual means when all material help had failed.

Someone had told her about a spiritual healer. He did not give medicines or drugs. He had no system of physical treatment. He asked her no questions about her symptoms, aches or pains, but sat meditatively by her and said, "Let us think about God and His wonders." Then he affirmed out loud: "God is a loving, guiding Father, immediate and accessible, an intimate healing power. God is present as Living Spirit and His Holy Presence is flowing into all parts of your being."

A remarkable change had taken place as she opened her mind and heart to the influx of the Holy Spirit. Her realization of the Infinite Healing Presence and her receptivity had caused a resurrection of wholeness, vitality and perfection, and a wonderful healing had followed. This is the power of the Spirit, or God. The turning point had come when she had realized that infinite resources of Divine love and wisdom were ready at hand within her.

A Simple Truth

The power of the Spirit (God) is not a half-way measure. We must carry the spiritual life into every sphere of our natural and social interests. We are here to live by the Spirit. God is Spirit, and this Spirit has become manifest in this beautiful world of time and space. This Spirit in us gives us the power to be victorious. There is in us a Divine Presence enabling us to lift our problems into heavenly light and see them transfigured by the guidance we claim and receive. There is a guidance for every need; there is love for each heart. Love is the greatest healing power, touching the subconscious, quickening, strengthening and transforming us into radiating centers which bless mankind.

Divine Love Heals

After speaking in London a few months ago, I had a conference with a woman who told me that all of a sudden she had suffered from glandular inflammation and her tissues had swollen badly. She was taking medicine and stated that the inflammation would sub-side for a few weeks, and then the condition would recur.

I asked her about her emotional life, pointing out that glands secrete hormones, and the word hormones means harmony. This woman revealed that she hated her sister, who had cheated her out of a large sum of money, and this hatred and hostility had caused the inflammation of her glands and other organs. In other words, she was imbibing poison.

The explanation was that she had to absorb and imbibe Divine love into her soul, which would restore her to harmony and wholeness. All religions teach the practice of love and goodwill to all and that we must love one another. In holistic medicine today, doctors insist that love and goodwill, as well as forgiveness, are definite necessities for health and happiness.

Accordingly, she decided to release her sister and heal herself. I explained to her that she did not have to mentally coerce or force herself to love her sister, as that procedure would bring about the law of reversed effort. All she had to do was to fill her soul, or subcon-scious, with Divine love.

Her prayer was: "God's healing love fills my whole being. God loves me and cares for me. God's river of peace saturates my whole being." She affirmed these truths for 20 minutes at a time, three times a day. She also followed my advice, which was that whenever the thought of her sister crossed her mind, she was to affirm: "God's love fills my soul."

I had a wonderful letter from her a week ago, saying: "I am at peace. I no longer need medicine. When my sister comes to my mind, I am at peace. There is no sting there any more. I wish her well." This is the power of love. It dissolves everything unlike itself. If you are at peace and full of goodwill to all, your organs or nerves do not cry out in pain, nor will your stomach give you acute indigestion or ulcers.

A New Insight Changed His Life

During a recent lecture tour in Europe, where I gave seminars in Munich, Frankfurt, Hanover, Zurich, Vienna and London, I met many interesting and outstanding people in the fields of science, medicine, business and politics. A highly placed government official visited me at my hotel in Munich, Germany, saying that he owed his success and advancement to practicing what he had read in *The Power of Your Subconscious Mind,* * which has been published in German for many years.

He said that he had had a rather low position and had been inadequately paid. He realized after reading my book that he had been given to criticizing, condemning and belittling others who had been promoted

*See *The Power of Your Subconscious Mind* by Dr. Joseph Murphy. Prentice-Hall, Inc., Englewood Cliffs, N.J., 1963.

into higher echelons. In so doing, he realized that he was also demoting himself. He said that he had stopped doing it and had learned to bless them, understand them, appreciate them for what they had accomplished, and decided from that point on to cooperate and get along with them as they were. He continued, saying that he had found that in blessing others and rejoicing in their promotion and advancement, he was also blessing himself. He then told me that he was here to thank me for writing the book.

This was one of the nicest tributes I received on my journey. Love is the universal solvent, and when you ask yourself honestly: Would I like to live with what I am thinking and wishing for the other person? and if the answer is yes, you are building health, happiness, prosperity and success into your own mentality. The reason is very simple: You are the only thinker in your world, and your thought is creative. Whatever you think about the other person, you are also creating in your own life.

The Inner Meaning of the Golden Rule Is Important

The Golden Rule is known to almost everyone, but how many understand what it really means? To put it in simple, everyday language, all it means is that whatever you think about another person you are creating in your own life, because your thought is creative. Knowing this to be true, you will be careful to think only God-like thoughts about the other. Every thought tends to manifest itself.

What a different world it would be if all of us practiced the Golden Rule and the law of love. We would create heaven on earth. The average man can quote the Golden Rule by heart, but he does not really understand the inner meaning of it. Therefore, he does not obey it.

And as ye would that men should do to you, do ye also to them likewise (Luke 6:31). This is a directive from within your own soul, which, when followed, brings harmony, health and peace into the lives of all who practice it. If people practiced the Golden Rule there would be no war, no crime, no cruelty, no rape, no suffering and no inhumanity. There would be no need for armies, navies, air forces, police, nor atomic or other nuclear weapons. When your thought is right, your action will be right. It is impossible to produce right action out of a negative thought, in the same way that you cannot get an apple tree from a non-viable seed.

He Said, "I Tried, but I Can't"

An alcoholic boasted to me that he had power to take a drink or two and then quit. It was an idle boast, as he was under compulsion to take another and another until he was drunk. His subconscious said one thing and his conscious mind said another. He was incapable because he was under a subconscious compulsion to drink. He had lost control. He was living under the compulsion of his habit and conditioned emotions. He was compelled from within.

He said to me that he took several drinks to give himself courage and lift his spirits. Each time he did this, however, he was rejecting his own Divinity, which is Omnipotent and All-Wise. He got what we call a false courage, a temporary lift, which was transitory. After repeating these suggestions of weakness, inferiority and inadequacy over and over again, these were impressed in his subconscious mind, and what is impressed on the subconscious is compulsive. Now he was an alcoholic, an inebriate, a compulsive drinker.

How He Reconditioned His Mind

This man learned that he had to develop an emotional backing for freedom or he would fail. He desired a healing, and every night prior to sleep he lulled himself with these words: "Freedom and peace of mind." As he continued to affirm freedom and peace of mind, he knew that he would establish a new habit.

After a few weeks he was compelled to sobriety and peace of mind. The same law that had taken him to the bottle had given him freedom and a perfect healing.

She Learned the Secret

A few months ago I gave a seminar in Vienna, Austria. During a conversation with an outstanding golfer, she disclosed that after learning all the rules and the techniques of playing, she said to herself every night: "I am relaxed, I am poised, I am serene, and I am calm before every game, and the Almighty Power within me takes over. I play majestically and gloriously. I play for Him."

She had studied the game from all angles, practiced regularly and disciplined her mind and body; but she was smart enough to let her Higher Self govern her hands, stance and direction in its own superior and inimitable way. She saturated her subconscious every night with the right words.

After a certain amount of repetition, she succeeded in impregnating her subconscious and she was compelled to be the great and outstanding golfer. The law of the subconscious is compulsive.

... That Ye Love One Another ... (John 13:34)

The inside governs the outside. You can't love others unless you have loving and harmonious thoughts in your mind. The people who inhabit your mind are thoughts, ideas, beliefs, opinions and your reactions to everyday events. Be sure they conform to whatsoever things are true, lovely, noble and Godlike.

Your disciples and the disciples mentioned in your Bible represent the disciplined qualities of your mind. Are you disciplining your vision? Your vision is what you are focussed on, what you are looking at in your own mind. And you go where your vision is. Your faith is disciplined when you adhere to and give allegiance to the creative laws of your mind and when you believe implicitly in the goodness of God in the land of the

64

living. Your faith is not in creeds, dogmas, traditions, men or institutions, but in the eternal principles, which are the same yesterday, today and forever.

You discipline your imagination when you imagine what is lovely and of good report. Your judgment, when disciplined, means you decide upon the truth or falsity of any thought. When you affirm the good constantly, that is called righteous judgment and brings harmony and peace into your life. Whatever you make real you will demonstrate on the screen of space.

Remember, if your mind is full of fear, worry, resentment, prejudices, anger, jealousy or religious bias, then you cannot really love because the occupants of your mind are the opposite of love. You project your mental attitude upon others and you will blame them and criticize them.

He Said that the Explanation Changed His Life

In the month of August, 1979, I spoke in Caxton Hall, London, and said to a troubled man, "You must preach the gospel to yourself. The moneychangers and thieves that you are talking about are in your own mind. You are the temple of consciousness, and the thieves and moneychangers which rob you are fear, ignorance, superstition, self-condemnation, self-criticism and ill will. The spiritually minded man casts all of these thieves and robbers out of his mind by filling his subconscious mind with life-giving patterns and the eternal truths of God. Then he will experience peace and harmony within and confidently express it without, in his body, his business, and in his relationships with all people."

This man had been thinking of a temple which existed 2000 years ago and believed the thieves and moneychangers to be outside of his own mind. Realizing that he was robbing himself of vitality, peace, harmony, wealth and success, he stopped doing it. A light seemed to come into his mind, penetrating the fog. The explanation was the cure.

Join Up With the Infinite

Recently I talked with a man who had said he felt guilty if he did not keep going. He had a sort of compulsion to keep on working even after a full day in the office. He was a "workaholic." He would bring home material and work until midnight on figures, plans and business projects. He had had two heart attacks as well as bleeding ulcers, all due to ulcerated thoughts and emotional upheavals.

He had forgotten that God had ordained the Sabbath—not as a day of the week, but as a time of mental rest where you may tune in with the Infinite, claiming frequently: "Infinite Spirit leads and guides me in all my ways. God's river of peace saturates my mind and heart."

I suggested to him that every evening he set aside some time for prayer and meditation, such as reading and meditating on the 91st, 23rd, 27th, 46th and 42nd

Psalms, alternating from time to time. He realized that he should turn regularly to the Source of strength, inspiration and quiet moments in the contemplation of God and His love, which would work wonders in his life.

He began meditating during his lunch hour, as well as every morning, on the great truths of *Quiet Moments with God** and discovered that he was completely released from the tension-making activities and anxieties of the day. Don't forget to call regularly and systematically on the wisdom of God to anoint your intellect and the power of the Almighty to strengthen you. Take five or ten minutes two or three times a day to dwell on the great truths of God; then you are practicing the Sabbath, which is to surrender to God and let an influx of the Holy Spirit invade and nourish your mind and body.

This man started to invite the Infinite Spirit within him to participate in all of his undertakings, and he discovered that his Senior Partner—his Higher Self—revealed to him better ways to do all things.

Your Desire Must Reach Your Subconscious

Many people have said to me that they wished for prosperity, success and the good things of life, and they prayed for a quiet and relaxed life, but nothing

---

*See *Quiet Moments with God* by Dr. Joseph Murphy, DeVorss and Company, Inc., Marina del Rey, Ca., 1958 (Twelfth Printing, 1978).

happened. Oftentimes they are so restless, fearful and habitually anxious that their routine thinking has become their master.

The way to overcome this is to think quietly about your desire for promotion, expansion, prosperity and success, realizing that your desire for growth and expansion is from God and that the power of the Almighty is bringing your desire to pass in Divine law and order. Gradually, as you think along these lines, you will succeed in integrating your desire in your subconscious mind, which will bring it to pass.

Many people in offices, factories and business establishments are more or less mechanical men and women, merely responding to the pressures and suggestions all around them. In this way, they tend to become automatons by responding to every wind that blows. Many are repeating the wrong thing, both in thought and action. Be sure to repeat to yourself the eternal verities. By repetition, faith and expectancy, you will reap a rich harvest.

He Had the Wrong Self-Image

In counselling a young man whose basic problem was that he was chronically ill, it became apparent that as soon as he recovered from one ailment he acquired another sickness. He had had six operations in six years. He maintained an image of himself as being sick. He had been told when he was young that he was sickly and would always be weak. He accepted this and, as a result, learned to be unhealthy. His belief that he was always destined to be sickly was in his subconscious mind, and whatever he believed came to pass.

Under my direction, he reversed this image and practiced the mirror treatment every morning for about five or ten minutes. He looked in the mirror and affirmed out loud: "I AM all health. God is my health." Gradually, the idea of wholeness entered into his subconscious mind, and he is now free from a false belief. He practiced the technique I gave him diligently and faithfully until it manifested in his life.

She Was Hounded by Fears and Guilt

A young woman 22 years of age said to me, "I am hounded by all kinds of fear." She was afraid of God, of the future, of the after life, of evil entities, of a devil and of voodoo. The Bible says: *For God hath not given us the spirit of fear; but of power, and of love, and of a sound mind* (II Timothy 1:7).

I explained to her that when young, we are all highly impressionable and malleable and that her parents and those around her had conditioned her mind with falsehoods about God, life and the universe. She began to realize that she was not born with any fears, sense of guilt or self-condemnation, and that all these had been given to her. She possessed weird ideas about

69

evil entities and beliefs that the woods were full of goblins and sprites. Danger seemed to lurk everywhere.

She began to read and meditate on the 27th Psalm* night and morning and began to affirm many times a day: "God loves me and cares for me. I am a daughter of God and a child of Eternity." She practiced this simple affirmation doggedly and faithfully, and she found a new estimate of herself, a new blueprint of herself. With this healthy vision of herself, she is blossoming forth in Divine order.

The Two Selves in You

Think along these lines: The first self is that which I now am; the second self is that which I long to be. Therefore, I must die psychologically to what I am so that I can live to that which I long to be. The above-mentioned girl died to the old self. All the falsehoods implanted in her mind in childhood were obliterated and she bequeathed all the energy she had locked up in the old beliefs to the new image of herself. The energy lost in her image of limitation, lack and fear passed over to the new image of success, charm and beauty.

*See *Songs of God. An Interpretation of My Favorite Psalms.* by Dr. Joseph Murphy. DeVorss & Co., Marina del Rey. Ca.. 1979.

THE POWER OF THE SPIRIT

The Road to Success

A young musician in Vienna told me of his struggle to reach what he called the top echelons of music. He said the opposition to his advancement, his poverty and lack of connections were a great handicap to him in the beginning. He had heard a lecture on the mind, however, and had begun to realize that the challenges, difficulties, impediments and delays which he had encountered had helped him to discover the powers within him. He had called on the Unseen Power, God, within him.

The odds were great against his rise, but he had kept on, repeating to himself that Infinite Intelligence opened up the way and that his sense of oneness with the Infinite would overcome all obstacles. All the challenges and setbacks had sharpened his mental and spiritual tools. His mother had had him read about Chopin, saying to him that his biography would give him strength. Apparently, it had given him the courage to keep on keeping on.

Chopin had been very ill and very poor, but he had had faith and confidence that there was a Power which would enable him to put the urges and dreams of his heart into manifestation. He had succeeded in composing 54 mazurkas and a great number of polonaise and many Polish songs. Infinite Spirit within him revealed the way. Though he was slowly passing on to the next dimension of life, he nevertheless fulfilled his heart's desire.

The old aphorism is still true: "Things live by moving, and they gain strength as they go." Paul says: *. . . For when I am weak, then am I strong* (II Corinthians 12:10). Give yourself wholly up to God; then nothing hinders His power from being made perfect in you. You are then strong. . . . *The Lord stood with me, and strengthened me* (II Timothy 4:17).

CHAPTER 5

Teach Us to Pray

An ancient expression says: "True prayer is not imposing sound that clamorous lips repeat, but the deep silence of a soul that clasps Jehovah's feet." Faith finds its appropriate and natural manifestation in prayer. There are the prayer of form and ritual and the prayer of faith and love. These are essentially different in their nature and effects.

Millions of people all over the world pray because it is a part of their religious life that they are trying to express, or they may pray from a sense of duty, looking upon it as a sort of task imposed upon them. In the prayer of faith and love, it is no longer a task or duty but a spiritual necessity in order to grow, expand and express health and happiness. Prayer could be looked upon as turning to the mercy seat within based on an irresistible Divine attraction. Prayer is communion with the Indwelling God—the Living Spirit Almighty —which is the Reality of every person.

On one occasion, it is said, as Jesus prayed, . . . *The fashion of his countenance was altered, and his raiment was white and glistening* (Luke 9:29). In the parallel passage in another of the Gospels, it is said that . . . *His face did shine as the sun, and his raiment was white as the light* (Matthew 17:2). Such spiritual transformations, in a degree, have been experienced by many other people throughout the world.

How She Experienced an Illumination

A few minutes prior to writing this chapter, I counselled with a psychiatric nurse, who told me that while she was meditating on the 23rd Psalm, together with a mental patient, her whole being was flooded by a radiant light accompanied by an ecstasy of the Spirit. This experience changed her whole life, and she is now studying to be a minister of the laws of mind and the way of the Spirit. The patient felt the Divine transfusion and was completely healed of a psychotic mentality.

In their mental and spiritual communion with God, many others have had similar experiences. God is Infinite Life, and such intimate fellowship with the primal source of our being influences and pours out Its wholeness, beauty and perfection upon our whole being.

The Holy of Holies

You can make contact with the Infinite through the medium of your thought. You can sit down quietly and think of God as boundless love, infinite intelligence, absolute harmony, indescribable beauty and absolute joy and dwell on these attributes and qualities. As you do this, you will experience a transfusion of God's grace and an effulgence of light and love. In this way you are the Holy of Holies—the Presence of God within you. All creeds and liturgies, as well as intercessors, are removed and you experience your personal fellowship with God.

The Prayer of Faith

The Bible says: . . . *The prayer of faith shall save the sick, and the Lord shall raise him up.* . . (James 5:15). There is no time or space in mind or Spirit. True prayer for a sick person does not consist of supplication or flowery words addressed to the Deity, nor a series of nicely wrought statements projected from unfeeling lips in the direction of the throne of God, which fall short of the mark. True prayer for the sick person is to claim earnestly and feelingly that the uplifting, healing, strengthening power of the Infinite Healing Presence is flowing through the patient, making him whole and perfect. Know and feel that the harmony, beauty and Life of God manifest themselves in him or her as peace, vitality, wholeness and perfection. Get a clear realization of this, and the sick condition will then dissolve in the light of God's love.

Paul says: . . . *Glorify God in your body* . . . (I Corinthians 6:20). Make sure that your mental picture agrees with your affirmation. In your mind's eye, you see the patient radiant, happy, joyous and bubbling over with life and love. That would be true prayer. True prayer is claiming that what is true of God is true of the person you are helping.

There is the type of prayer that cannot be "worded," since prayer becomes oftentimes more efficacious in proportion to the degree it becomes more internal. It is simply turning to the God-Presence within and opening your heart to receive the influx of His healing currents and Divine love. True prayer, when uttered, is radiant with love and spiritual life. Look upon true prayer as carrying a Divine fragrance from the God-Presence in you, and when wafted upon the ill person, it has a life-giving spiritual potency in it. The subconscious of the sick person is stimulated and reinforced and proceeds to resurrect God's omnipotent love. A healing then follows.

. . . *The effectual fervent prayer of a righteous man availeth much* (James 5:16). It is in accordance with the laws of mind, unbending and invariable spiritual laws, that sincere, earnest prayer for the sick affects them and helps in the restoration of perfect health. If one should rise instantly and walk, or be raised to newness of life, in response to prayer, it would be no miracle, no violation of the laws of mind.

How She Prayed for Her Brother-in-Law

An old friend of mine in Pasadena, California, prayed for her brother-in-law, who had suffered a severe fall and fractured his pelvis. He was taken to the hospital and, because of his age, the physicians believed not much could be done for him. She decreed feelingly and knowingly that God walks and talks in him and that God's healing love was flowing through him. She imagined him standing in front of her in her home telling her about the miracle of healing which had taken place. She saw him smiling and radiant. She did this frequently, over and over again.

In a short period of time, he arose out of bed, walked around in the hospital, came home and confirmed objectively what she had imagined and claimed to be true subjectively in the silence of her soul. That was true prayer.

The Promises of God

The promises of God could be called the laws of God, which are the same yesterday, today and forever. These promises do not belong to the dead past but to the living present. The existence of God is an eternal now. In Divine mind, past, present and future are all one. All existence is included in the Divine moment— the Eternal Now.

As there is no future in God, the promise of God is not a pledge to give us something at some remote day; it is based on our acceptance of our good now, this present moment.

Look at everyday money transactions. You accept a check or bank note for money, yet it is not money, only a piece of paper. It is a promise to pay dollars on demand. Likewise, there is in the Divine promise the blessing for which we ask. Warren Evans, a great healer and a student of Phineas Parkhurst Quimby, said: "Whatever we hope, by faith we have, future and past subsisting now."

The Bible says: . . . *In him we live, and move, and have our being.* . . (Acts 17:28). God is the Life Principle in us and is the source of our health, peace and all the blessings of life. Here is the inspired utterance of Charles Wesley:

> The well of life to us thou art,
> Of joy the swelling flood;
> Wafted by thee, with willing heart
> We swift return to God.

You Are a Mediator

There are many practitioners, doctors, clergymen and others whose presence generates a mental and physical healing. They are charged with power from On High and their healing atmosphere is veritably contagious. They prove to be a tower of strength to the weak and infirm, and sick people are affected by them far and near.

The true idea of a physician is that of a doctor or teacher, as the word implies. In the highest sense, he is one who can "minister to minds diseased." There have been men like Dr. Quimby, Warren Evans and others in the early days of our country who searched for the hidden haunts of the seeds of disease in the mental conditions of the patient. Today we would call them clairvoyant, as, without talking to the patients, they could reveal the hidden cause of the sickness before the patient said a word. Oftentimes, the explanation was the cure.

Angels Watch Over You

Many people have asked me about angels. The word *angel* means the angle at which you look at God. It also means an attitude of mind, an inspiration, or a message from your Higher Self. The Bible says: *And there appeared an angel unto him from heaven, strengthening him* (Luke 22:43). *. . . Angels came and ministered unto him* (Matthew 4:11).

All of us are angels of God in another way of looking at it. When we pass on to the next dimension, we are still angels, or expressions of God, operating in a rarefied and attenuated body. Your loved ones are all around you, separated by frequency only. It is unequivocally stated in the 91st Psalm,* *There shall no evil befall thee, neither shall any plague come nigh thy dwelling. For he shall give his angels charge over thee, to keep thee in all thy ways* (Psalms 91:10-11).

The Infinite Presence responds to each person according to the law of reciprocal relationship. In the

---

*See *Songs of God: An Interpretation of My Favorite Psalms,* by Dr. Joseph Murphy, DeVorss & Co., Marina del Rey, Ca., 1979.

highest sense of the term, prayer is contact with the God-Presence within, Whose nature is responsiveness. There are many people all over the world praying to saints and angels. In the hour of their extremity, they are speaking in the language of Hamlet: "Angels and ministers, defend us!"

Saints represent any man or woman dedicated to the truths of God, and who practices the Presence of God. In other words, it means any person who entertains God-like thoughts and walks in paths of righteousness. The invocation of saints and angels has been practiced by millions of people all over the world. These represent good men and women who led God-like lives.

A man in India once said to me that he addresses holy men in the next dimension as living beings, living in a higher realm of mind, namely the fourth dimension. He asks their aid, their prayers and their intercession with God. Because of his faith and belief, he gets results. Whether the object of your faith be true or false, you will get results, for according to your faith is it done unto you. Your subconscious responds to your blind faith. His faith and confidence and his belief that the holy men would respond to him was accepted by his subconscious mind and, of course, his prayers were answered.

People all over the world have had remarkable healings by calling on saints and angels long since gone. But if you reason it out, they have not gone any place.

They are all around you, functioning fourth-dimensionally, just like your relatives who have passed on.

All good must come from God, the primal source of all blessings. Millions theorize that it is perfectly proper to ask dedicated souls in the next dimension of life for help in times of extremity. If to ask a spiritual healer or a dedicated doctor to aid and help you involves nothing objectionable and is not robbing God of the worship due Him, why is it improper to ask the same dedicated man who is now in a higher realm of mind to aid us after he has graduated to a higher world? All these forms of prayer get results, also. . . . *If thou canst believe, all things are possible to him that believeth* (Mark 9:23).

Are You Omnipresent?

A Yogi at the Forest University, Ashram at Rishikesh, which is at the foot of the Himalaya Mountains, said to me that many people ask him if they request aid of those in the next dimension, is it possible that they hear them, or are they in different lands, with omnipresence only applying to God? He explained to them that to be present in 15,000 places is not omnipresence. Spirit (God) is out of the limitations of time and space. This is the distinction between Spirit and matter. He added that when he speaks in India to thousands of people, he is present to all of them through the medium of sight and sound. A man who writes a book, by his thoughts and beliefs, is present to

81

millions of readers all over the world through the medium of his book. Therefore, he said, it may be easily conceived that those holy people in the next dimension are present by their thoughts and their love, which constitute their essential life, to a great many people and places at the same time, through spiritual law.

The old aphorism states: "The saints on Earth, and all the dead, but one communion make." There is really no separation, since subjectively we are all one. The word *humanity* means the One appearing as many.

Nearer to Thee

It is God who . . . *giveth to all life, and breath, and all things* (Acts 17:25). The nearer you get to the Infinite Presence within you, the more you will have of life, love and all good things. You will draw all the spiritual nutrition you need from the heart of Infinite love and life.

Is It Wise?

Many point out rather wisely that the invocation of the saints and angels, who are referred to as holy men, living in the next dimension may be best illustrated in this way: that a particle of dust in the eye will obscure and hide from us the sun in the heavens. It is not wise or prudent that saints and angels should attract more attention and devotion than God, the source of all blessings.

I look upon all these approaches as good, however, in the sense that they are meeting levels of consciousness. In their own way, they are turning to the light.

The Patron Saint

Many cities have their patron saint, who is the most prominent object of veneration and adoration. Unillumined people give more attention to saints and angels than to God, the Father of all. The ancient gods of Greece and Rome were only deified men, as Cicero expressly affirms in his writings. These gods represented a ladder by means of which many were lifted up to the conception and realization of the Supreme God. In all these cases, we must remember that people are turning to what they conceive to be a higher power. They are, in their own way, seeking a higher power.

The Bible says: *Ask, and it shall be given you; seek, and ye shall find; knock, and it shall be opened unto you; for every one that asketh receiveth; and he that seeketh findeth; and to him that knocketh, it shall be opened* (Matthew 7:7-8). Prayer should form a part of all healing processes. . . . *Pray one for another, that ye may be healed. . .* (James 5:16).

But it must be prayer in its all-encompassing mood of faith and love, causing the God Presence to respond as vitality, wholeness and perfection. Time and space vanish before the power of Spirit. All individuals are included in the one great unity of pure Spirit (God) and are bound together, for God is all and is in all.

You Can Build A Glorious Future

The prophet Hosea said a wonderful thing: "Take your thoughts to God." This is a very practical and simple approach, and habitually following this direction transforms our lives. The thoughts we habitually think form grooves, or impressions, in our deeper mind. The Spirit, or Life Principle, responds and creates in our experience according to the tracks laid down in our subconscious mind. God is to us what we conceive God to be.

I said to a businessman who was failing in business and in health that he should stop building a prison in his mind. He said to me that he had no imagination. I explained to him that imagination was the first faculty of man and that everybody has imagination and is using it all the time, for good or for ill. According to the way in which he uses his imagination, so does he become and so does he act.

He had been building a mental prison by blaming his difficulties on others, the government, relatives and business associates. He began to see, however, that he was the propagator of his own problems. He began to take responsibility for his life, and he decided to take his thoughts to God within himself. He began to constantly affirm: "My business is God's business, and God is prospering me now. God guides and directs me. God's peace fills my soul. God is my boss and my guide, and God's healing love saturates my whole being."

He kept reiterating these truths to himself many times a day and gradually he eradicated the hundred and one vexations and contentions lurking in his mind. In his own words, he got the world, its news and its crime off his shoulders, and he no longer hates, resents and condemns all those around him. He is building a glorious future by taking his thoughts to God, as suggested by Hosea thousands of years ago.

You Are the Captain on the Bridge

The captain directs the ship. He does not feel that he is a victim of the seas or is at the mercy of the waves. He understands the principle of navigation and controls and directs his destiny, moving towards his goal in life. He does not worry, fret and fuss about chance, fate or accidents. He plans for victory at all times.

You are created to win, to triumph, to conquer. You should never dwell upon failure, loss, lack or limitation of any kind. To do so is to build a prison in your mind, thereby leading a limited and circumscribed life, a sort of miserable existence. You are placed here to go forward and never retreat.

Napoleon said that "imagination rules the world." He became a famous general and a marvelous strategist. He imagined victory and focussed his mind exclusively on the triumphant end, becoming master of Europe.

Historians inform us that before the battle of Waterloo, he planned a retreat in case he lost the battle or the battle tide turned against him. He had to use it because he built a retreat in his mind, and that which he greatly feared came upon him, just as Job had pointed out thousands of years ago.

Another interesting aspect in the life of Napoleon was that he held in great awe and respect any man with a long nose. This was a sort of superstitious belief. In all probability, the belief went back to his childhood when some relative had told him that men with long noses had some superhuman qualities and were Divinely gifted with extraordinary insights and wisdom. In other words, he transferred the power within himself to men with long noses. He created failure in his own mind and he experienced it, for Wellington, who defeated him, had a very large nose.

. . . *There is no power but of God; the powers that be are ordained of God* (Romans 13:1).

Age Is Not the Flight of Years

There are numerous people living here in Leisure World, Laguna Hills, who pay no attention to years. Many are very active at 90 and over. They not only indulge in all the various recreational activities, but are also quite active in their professional capacities and contribute much to the health and cultural activities in the area. They do not subscribe to the belief that the accumulation of years brings on deafness, poor eyesight or physical deterioration. They realize the Spirit never grows old and never dies.

The statistics given out by insurance companies regarding old age do not refer to any law of life. They refer to the general mass belief. They have established certain rules but the exception proves the rule. A rule made by man is not a law of life. When you see people 90 to 95 years of age driving their cars, wearing no glasses or hearing aids, this proves that the transcendent man resides in all of us.

He's a Medical Marvel

The following article was published in the *National Enquirer*, July 31, 1979:

He's a Medical Marvel
160-Year-Old Man Still Works & Smokes
Up to 100 Cigarettes a Day

At 160, Manoel de Moura of Brazil may well be the oldest man in the world.

While many wild claims of old age have been debunked in recent years, Manoel not only has his birth certificate to prove his age, but also the testimony of people who are themselves now very old—and remember him as an old man when they were children!

"When I was a young boy, Manoel was already an old man, pushing 100," recalled Teodoro Boskow, former vice mayor of the town of Cerrito Alegre, who's now in his 80s. "He looks the same now as he did 70 years ago—except that now he's a little hunchbacked."

Modesta Lemos, 70, told the ENQUIRER: "When we were just beginning school, Manoel was a very old man with that same white hair and beard."

The mystery of Manoel's extreme age is deepened by the fact that a local doctor, who's the only doctor Manoel has ever seen, can find absolutely nothing wrong with him.

"This is the most incredible thing I have ever seen—not only in my medical career, but in my life," declared general practitioner Francisco Luz.

"The health of this 160-year-old man is supernormal. His blood pressure is normal, and his heart beats exactly like the heart of a 20-year-old man. Medicine has no answer to explain his longevity. . ."

Manoel's birth certificate says he was born March 25, 1819, in a rural town in Brazil. The document speaks for itself.

"There is no doubt about Manoel's age," concluded Theofilo Salamao, City Councilman in the town of Pelotas. "The birth certificate was given to him by the State of Rio Grande do Sul of the Federal Republic of Brazil."

Manoel, who has spent most of his life as a farm laborer, attributes his remarkably well-preserved condition to simple living.

"My key to survival is the land," he told The ENQUIRER. "I have lived my entire life working the land, making things grow. I have been to the movies only once. I saw television once, but I didn't understand what was going on.

"I don't own anything, and I don't worry about anything, either."

Adding to the puzzle of Manoel's strapping good health is his habit of chain-smoking.

"I could smoke all day if I had enough cigarettes," he said. "Usually I smoke between 80 and 100 cigarettes a day."

Manoel's employer, Ary Lemos, feeds the old man and gives him shelter in return for his labor.

"Manoel is the best worker I've ever had. Most of the kids around here are lazy, but Manoel is a dedicated worker.

"He cuts wood, hoes the soil, plants, clears the fields. His eyesight is perfect—he can thread a needle on the first try."

The Brazilian government last month finally got around to granting Manoel a retirement pension of $25 a month for as long as he lives.

But the money doesn't impress the old man,

who has no living relatives and has never been married.

"What I enjoy most out of life," he grinned, "is just a hot cup of coffee and a cigarette."

—by Michael J. Hoy

Her Religion Was Her Problem

A young woman about 22 years of age came to see me. She was what she termed very religious. She didn't dance, play cards, drink wine or go to the movies, neither did she date men. She went to church every morning and followed all the rules and tenets of her religion.

She was suffering from what her doctor had told her was anxiety neuroses. She was taking tranquilizers and pills to reduce her high blood pressure. She was mad at God for permitting all these things to happen to her.

I explained to her that true religion is of the heart and not of the lips, and that while she was conventionally good in following all the rules, rites and ceremonies of her sectarian beliefs, her false concept of God and her grotesque belief that God was punishing her caused all her mental and emotional problems.

She finally began to realize she was her own persecutor and tormentor. There is the old aphorism: "He who discovers himself loses his misery." She discovered that her negative thinking had been the cause of all her problems and the explanation was the cure. She decided to make it a habit to think right, feel right, and act right according to universal principles and eternal verities.

Remember ye not the former things, neither consider the things of old (Isaiah 43:18). . . . *Behold, I make all things new. . .* (Revelation 21:5).

CHAPTER 6

Becoming Spiritual-Minded

Many people have a vague idea of what it is to be spiritual. To become spiritual-minded, according to the beliefs of many people, is confused with conforming to certain devotions, rituals and ceremonies. What is it to become spiritual? How may I become so? These are questions of great importance to all men and women.

You will become spiritual-minded when you make up your mind to think heavenly thoughts, which means to think according to eternal verities and principles of life, which are the same yesterday, today and forever. Your subconscious mind is the seat of habit, and as you continue thinking God-like thoughts, you will form a very good habit and wonders will happen in your life.

The Bible says: *Judge not according to the appearance, but judge righteous judgment* (John 7:24). To judge is to separate that which is false from that which is true. In other words, you come to a decision in your mind regarding the truth or falsity of any thought. To affirm the good and the true is righteous judgment and brings harmony and peace into your life.

If a man is sick or crippled, you don't deny the evidence of your senses, but you go to the Infinite Healing Presence within you and affirm wholeness, vitality and perfection for him. You see him as he ought to be: happy, joyous and free. Your interpretation of what your five senses report to you may be wrong. Check on how you interpret what your senses report to you.

Many people think that in order to be spiritual-minded, they must put in practice ascetic mortifications, which are really of no value. Instead, to develop spiritually, you start from the inside, not the outside. As you spiritualize your thought life, your body will magically melt into the image and likeness of your contemplation.

You Can Rise

And I, if I be lifted up from the earth, will draw all men unto me (John 12:32). Lift up your concept of God and realize that the Holy of Holies is within yourself. As you dwell upon the attributes and qualities of God within yourself, the more your spiritual power and psychological force are augmented. Just so far as we know God, do we become more God-like, and we can do Divine works to the same extent.

Affirm frequently: "I exalt God in the midst of me, mighty to heal and restore. I am illumined from On

High." Make a habit of this and you will find that you are lifted up and inspired to accomplish great things. Be careful not to subsequently deny what you affirm.

Begin to Believe

Belief and life, from an etymological standpoint, are the same. To believe is to live. To believe is a movement of our interior life towards the fulfillment of our desire. In other words, pour life and love into your ideal, goal or desire. Live in the state of being it. Live the role just like an actor or actress. Animate your desire. Contemplate its fulfillment and see the happy ending.

To believe that you are being healed or prospered now turns the current of Universal Life in that direction. Believe in the truths of the Spirit rather than in the evidence of your five senses. This is salvation in the complete signification of the word.

The Meaning of the Blood of the Lamb

In ancient times the mystics expressed and preserved the highest truths under the covering of appropriate symbols. In the zodiac, which signifies the circle or cycle of life, the first is Aries, the Lamb. The sun crosses the equator on the 21st of March, which is called the ingress of Aries, and it is said that it sheds its blood (actinic rays and heat) on the passover (as it passes over). All the seeds frozen in the ground are resurrected and we are saved from starvation. Following is a regeneration of all life in the northern latitudes.

If your mother is ill, you can shed your blood for her, symbolically speaking, by pouring life and love into the idea of wholeness, vitality and perfection for her and by imagining her to be whole, vital and strong. You are giving her the living truth of the Spirit, which means the shedding of your blood in symbolic language. Blood means Life. In this blood, which is perpetually shed for many sick people throughout the world, we wash our robes and make them white.

You may pray for an alcoholic or someone suffering from any other specific disease and the patient may get well; but you must also teach him the cause of his trouble and instruct him how to pray. Otherwise, he may have a relapse. Not to do so would be somewhat similar to a fireman who rushes into a burning building to rescue a trapped man and only seizes his clothes, leaving the man as he was.

The highest function of a healer is to serve as a doctor or teacher. The ancient meaning of doctor was that of a man who taught others about the Divinity within them, which enabled them to rise and overcome their passions and appetites and move onward, upward and Godward.

The ancient mystics said: "If that thou seekest and thou findest not within thee, thou wilt never find it without thee." When you pray for an invalid, you are mentally in tune with the Infinite Healing Presence within you. Since there is no time or space in the Infinite Spirit, you can accelerate the healing process in the invalid.

The Price You Pay

The price you pay for spiritual unfoldment is attention, recognition and devotion to the eternal truths of life. You pay with mental and spiritual coin. There is no free lunch, and attention is the key to life. As you absorb and mentally digest more and more of wisdom, truth and beauty, you will be able to impart the healing message to others.

You cannot give what you do not have; therefore, *. . . seek ye first the kingdom of God, and His righteousness* (right thinking); *and all these things shall be added unto you* (Matthew 6:33). Gold and silver in the Bible are symbols of celestial good and truth. As you look to the Source of all blessings, you are recognizing your everlasting inheritance and you will never want for any good thing.

Dr. Warren Evans wrote in 1884:

> Think truly, and thy thoughts
> Will the world's famine feed;
> Speak truly, and each word of thine
> Will be a fruitful seed;
> Live truly, and thy life will be
> A great and noble creed.

BECOMING SPIRITUAL-MINDED

Why He Was Disappointed

Recently I talked with a man who had been experiencing an acute business problem. He needed a loan from the bank to tide him over for some months, but due to recent restrictions he was turned down. He was very tense and anxious. He also understood that these negative emotions would generate the reverse of what he was praying for.

I suggested that he go to the Source of all blessings —namely, the Infinite Spirit within him—and affirm the great eternal truths to bring his mind to a state of peace and rest. I suggested that he detach his mind from the problem and assume an attitude of Divine indifference, which means that it is impossible for your prayer to fail. Infinite Intelligence knows only the answer.

I suggested also that he reiterate the following age-old truths, realizing that when his mind was at peace, the answer would come. Accordingly, he meditated on the following scriptural verses several times a day, and when fear thoughts came to him, he would immediately quote one of the verses to himself:

—*But my God shall supply all your need according to his riches in glory . . . (Philippians 4:19).*
—*In quietness and in confidence shall be your strength . . . (Isaiah 30:15).*
—*. . . God, who giveth us richly all things to enjoy (I Timothy 6:17).*

97

—. . . *But with God all things are possible* (Matthew 19:26).

—. . . *Before they call, I will answer; and while they are yet speaking, I will hear* (Isaiah 65:24).

—. . . *According to your faith be it unto you* (Matthew 9:29).

—. . . *If thou canst believe, all things are possible to him that believeth* (Mark 9:23).

—*He shall call upon me, and I will answer him: I will be with him in trouble; I will deliver him, and honour him* (Psalm 91:15).

—*All things be ready if the mind be so* (Shakespeare).

—*The Lord is my light and my salvation; whom shall I fear? . . .* (Psalm 27:1).

—*I will lift up mine eyes unto the hills, from whence cometh my help* (Psalm 121:1).

He remained faithful to his meditation, and one of his customers, to whom he had previously mentioned his predicament, suddenly came to him and generously advanced him far more money than he needed and his problem was solved. When he established a Divine indifference to results, the answer came. Contemplating these statements of the Law of Life frequently, he succeeded in building into his mentality a state of peace and equilibrium.

The Psalmist expressed it this way: *But his delight is in the law of the Lord; and in his law doth he meditate day and night* (Psalm 1:2). You induce a quiet, receptive mind as you reflect on the great truths, and you then will dramatize the answer more quickly.

How He Conquered Despondency

A young college student came to see me and told me that the girl to whom he had been engaged and was about to marry had been killed in one of the recent air crashes. He was failing in his studies and was depressed, dejected and suffering from melancholia. At the same time he was taking tranquilizers, but when the effect wore off, he was right back where he started.

I suggested to him that he must not let these negative emotions gel and crystalize in his subconscious mind, which would cause a very negative subconscious complex with harmful results. I explained to him that an expert motorist here in Leisure World had had a crackup while going 90 miles an hour. He had not been seriously injured, and while the Automobile Club truck was towing his car to the repair shop, he immediately called a taxi and drove around for about an hour or more, the reason being that he wanted to prevent that experience from forming a negative pattern in his subconscious. He did not want to develop a fear complex.

This young man began to realize that everyone eventually passes on to the next dimension and that his gloom and despondency were not helping his sweetheart in the next dimension of life, but were actually holding her back. He decided to loose her and let her go, affirming whenever he thought of her, "God gives you peace and harmony."

He then redirected his mind to his studies and began

to keep his mind tuned in to the Infinite Presence and Power, reflecting frequently on Divine guidance, peace and harmony. Following this procedure, his negative emotions were dissolved in the light of Divine love.

The Prince of This World

. . . For the prince of this world cometh, and hath nothing in me (John 14:30). A young college girl in a nearby university, who has read several of my books, including *Songs of God,** said to me that she had belonged to a certain cult and had since dropped the association when she realized that it was all rank superstition and balderdash. The other three members had told her that they would pour imprecations upon her and that she would suffer.

She knew that the prince of the world is fear and that their intention was to instill fear and terror into her mind, a sort of hypnotic suggestion. She read the inner meaning of the 91st Psalm and reiterated many passages during the day. Whenever the memory of their threat came into her mind, she would immediately affirm, "God loves me and cares for me."

She knew that if she could not give hate, she could not receive it. All she did was bless them and walk on, laughing at their dire predictions, knowing full well

---

*See *Songs of God* by Dr. Joseph Murphy, DeVorss and Company, Inc., Marina del Rey, California, 1979.

that they were negative suggestions which she refused to accept. Of course, the negative thoughts of her former friends boomeranged and were returned to them. All three, she told me, were subsequently killed in an auto crash.

The prince of this world (fear) had come to her and had found nothing in her to correspond to that fear. She knew the Law of Life. She had enthroned in her mind peace, harmony, right action and Divine love. The truths of the 91st Psalm had penetrated her subconscious and she walked with God, finding ways of pleasantness and paths of peace.

How to Handle Fear

It might be true to say that fear comes to everyone at some time, somewhere, in some way. The writer remembers that many years ago, while flying over the North Pole on the way to Norway and Sweden, a great storm had taken place. All of the passengers had been terrified. A few of us had begun to recite the 91st Psalm out loud, which had quieted them to some degree. They were afraid of death and destruction. That had been the only way to handle that group fear that had seized all of us.

Fear is contagious. Love is contagious, also. All of us must understand that no influence or suggestion from the external world can ever affect us unless it finds kinship with something inside of us. The girl previously referred to who had been threatened with a

HOW TO USE THE LAWS OF MIND

voodoo curse had rejected their suggestion because she knew it could not affect her unless she accepted it; and then it would be simply a movement of her own mind. This suggestion had found no home, no acceptance; therefore, it could not function and its force was dissipated.

As you continue to grow spiritually by absorbing and imbibing the great truths of life, you will be convinced that what the Psalmist said is true: *A thousand shall fall at thy side, and ten thousand at thy right hand; but it shall not come nigh thee* (Psalm 91:7). In verses 9 and 10 of the same Psalm,* we read: *Because thou hast made the Lord, which is my refuge, even the most High, thy habitation; there shall no evil befall thee, neither shall any plague come nigh thy dwelling.*

This is a very beautiful and definite promise. It points out that you will always be protected, directed and watched over by the spell of God's love. By pondering frequently the fact that God loves you and cares for you, guides you and directs you, you are making the most High your habitation. Because you constantly remind yourself that God's love surrounds you, enfolds you and enwraps you, you are always immersed in the Holy Omnipresence and no trouble can touch you.

*See *Songs of God* by Dr. Joseph Murphy. DeVorss and Company. Inc., Marina del Rey, California, 1979.

102

BECOMING SPIRITUAL-MINDED

There Is an Easier Way

A businessman said to me after a lecture a few Sundays ago, "I spent my early years toiling, moiling, and grabbing for the good things of life. I was always trying to make ends meet. I wanted more money, a home, a car and lovely surroundings."

He had gone to a spiritual counselor for advice, and she had told him that he was trying too hard. She taught him to go to the Source of all good—the God-Presence within—and to claim peace, harmony, right action, beauty and abundance. She told him that God was flowing through him, filling up all the empty vessels in his life.

He continued along that spiritual path, and all the things he had been seeking were added to him. His faith and confidence in the Infinite Presence within him were translatable to health, wealth, true expression and an abundant supply of money, also. He stopped trying so hard, begging and beseeching for the gifts of Life which have been proffered to all of us from the dawn of time.

Shakespeare said, "All things be ready if the mind be so." Open your mind to receive; learn to be a good receiver. God has given you Himself and the whole world. It is, therefore, foolish and stupid to beseech the Infinite to do something for us, because it is written, . . . *Before they call, I will answer; and while they are yet speaking, I will hear* (Isaiah 65:24). No matter what your problem is, the answer is there even before you ask.

The best spiritual medicine today is to get acquainted with the Spirit within you and then claim peace, harmony, and Divine law and order in your life. Reflect and dwell upon the Divine Law, which is: "I AM that which I contemplate." Contemplate whatsoever things are true, lovely, noble and God-like and let wonders happen in your life.

The Secrets of Life

The other evening I heard a psychologist speaking. Among other things, she said that man had perfected the laser beam, which now could destroy missiles in space. She also related its many other applications in medicine, the air industry and warfare. She said that we have split the atom and have broken the DNA code dealing with our genetic record, which determines the color of our skin, eyes and general physiognomy. We have isolated most of the hormones which are usually secreted by our glandular system and which keep our body in balance.

With all of this knowledge, she pointed out, we have not yet learned to live in peace and harmony. The answer to all of this is simple. The answer was given by the ancient mystic when he said, "When a man discovers himself, he loses his misery." The self of you is

God. The Bible says: *Acquaint now thyself with him and be at peace...* (Job 22:21).

The Answer to Doom and Gloom

We have a great number of prophets today predicting all manner of disasters, and they are instilling fear and uncertainty in the minds of millions of people. I counsel with many people who are morose, morbid, sullen and ill humored. They are afraid of old age, atomic warfare, insecurity and the future, and many are living in fear of death.

The Bible says: *... God hath not given us the spirit of fear; but of power, and of love, and of a sound mind* (II Timothy 1:7). It is true that fear, in some form, comes to all of us. When hearing the honk of a horn when walking along the road, you step aside, and the momentary fear is transmuted to desire to live, and you are free.

Many listen to the news and read the magazines and papers predicting nuclear war, the end of the world, earthquakes, etc. As they dwell on these predictions, they are seized with a sort of crippling fear.

I suggest to them that they hold these fears up to the light of reason, examine them and recognize that most of these predictions never come to pass, but come out of the fetid brain of the prognosticator of doomsday. Paul points out in Corinthians, *... Whether there be prophecies, they shall fail...* (I Corinthians 13:8).

Basically, all of this abnormal fear is due to a man's basic sense of insecurity, in failing to align himself with the Infinite Presence and Power. When he joins up with this Source, the Life Principle, which is all-powerful, all-wise and knows no opposition, he discovers a reflex action and his abnormal fear is gradually dissipated.

They Called Him the Rock of Gibraltar

A secretary once told me that the manager in the office where she worked was very domineering, arrogant, and boastful and treated the salesmen and the office girls rather shabbily. His mind was devoid of simplicity and his conversations were turgid. There was a cruel acerbity to his tongue.

The General Manager had visited the office and had found some things wrong. He had mildly reprimanded the manager; and this man, who had seemed to be so solid, unmoved and confident, cracked up and cried "like a baby." He had to go to the doctor for a sedative. Actually, his external demeanor and apparent confidence were a cover-up for a deep sense of insecurity, inadequacy and a profound inferiority complex.

A man who has faith and confidence in the Powers of the Infinite and who has self-esteem does not succumb to mild criticism. Actually, it acts as a stimulus to his confidence in himself. You become a true leader when you take command of the motley crew of thoughts in your own mind, dwelling on whatsoever things are true, honest, loving, noble and God-like.

This manager had a false estimate of himself and thought that by bluffing and blustering he could cover it up. To play the bully, to storm and to rage is a sure sign of a deep sense of inferiority. Braggadocio is empty and pretentious bragging. You will recall that the braggadocio of Mussolini and the megalomania of Hitler brought about their ultimate downfall.

Don't Compare Yourself With Others

God never repeats himself. You are unique, and there is no one in all the world like you. Many men and women who were timid, shy and retiring have visited me for counselling, and I have always pointed out to them the vast potentials within them waiting only to be called upon, resurrected and utilized. I explained to them that when fear came to their mind, it meant that they were supposed to call on the Divine reserves within them, thereby enabling them to overcome fear.

As they practice calling on the God Presence for guidance, strength and wisdom, they rise from that sense of inadequacy and keep going when others give up. One man, who had been born into poverty, told me that the reason he had reached the presidency of his company was due to his tremendous drive to overcome poverty and achieve his true place in life. His lack urged him on and acted as a powerful incentive to his ascent up the ladder of life.

Many women with an inferiority complex have told me that it was this sense of insecurity, inadequacy and inferiority which acted as their main driving force to excel, advance and go up the ladder of life. A formula which I have suggested to many women is as follows: Stand before the mirror every morning for five or ten minutes and affirm out loud: "I AM a daughter of the Infinite. I AM a child of eternity. My father is God, and God loves me."

As they keep using this prayer regularly every morning, it gradually sinks down by a process of mental and spiritual osmosis into their subconscious mind. This new concept of themselves, being impregnated in their deeper mind, comes forth and their whole life is transformed. The law is: What is impressed in the subconscious is expressed.

He Wanted to Become a Minister

Two years ago a young man who listens to my radio program asked me how he could become a minister of Divine Science. I suggested that he go and see Dr. Margaret Stevens, Santa Anita Church, Arcadia. She has a wonderful ministerial school there and has already graduated many men and women. The teachers are Professor Holland, Professor Bach, Dr. Stevens and many other outstanding metaphysical teachers.

BECOMING SPIRITUAL-MINDED

I met this young man last Sunday and he is still talking about taking up the ministry, claiming that is all that he really wants to do; however, he has done nothing about it. He has not inquired at or attended the school. In other words, he has not taken one step toward the realization of his heart's desire. He has not made an effort.

There are many people like that. They say, "I must take up Spanish or German, as it is very important in my business," yet, they have had ample opportunities to study these languages and have done nothing about it. They are simply daydreaming.

I know a man who has been talking about writing a book for over ten years regarding his extraordinary war experiences. I suggested to him several times that all he has to do is to sit down and write, and not wait for God to write. When he begins, God begins.

You are here to live life gloriously, so stop daydreaming. You are here to give your talents to the world and make it a better place to live in. This would-be writer shrinks and evades the effort to achieve and express himself in a wonderful way. All of us should listen to the admonition of the ancient Greek philosopher when he said, "The only proper study of man is man."

Law of Cause and Effect

Another way of explaining the law of cause and effect is to say that you are belief expressed. Whatever

109

your conscious mind really believes, your subconscious will bring forth.

I went into a business establishment recently, and the chief clerk told me that the business was going into bankruptcy. The reason he gave was that the owner had been leading a sort of double life. He had a mistress, was getting a divorce, and was ruthless with the clerks in the store. He was constantly changing help, because they resented the way he treated them.

Emerson said that every institution is a shadow of the man. His failure in business was really his complete failure in the art of living life successfully and harmoniously. His inner sense of guilt, his fear and inner conflicts, and his resentment toward his wife and others were the cause, not the business. Success depends on how you feel on the inside. The inside controls the outside. As within, so without.

A Better Future

. . . God hath not given us the spirit of fear, but of power, and of love, and of a sound mind (II Timothy 1:7).

Each day is a time of renewal, resurgence and rebirth. All nature proclaims the glory of a new day. This is to remind us that we must awaken the God within us and arise from our long winter sleep of limitation and walk forth into the morning of a new day and a new life. Fear, ignorance, and superstition must die in us and we must resurrect faith, confidence, love and goodwill.

Begin now to take the following transfusion of God's grace and love: "I am filled with the free-flowing, cleansing, healing, harmonizing, vitalizing life of the Holy Spirit. My body is the temple of the Living God, and it is pure, whole and perfect in every part. Every function of my mind and body is controlled and governed by Divine wisdom and Divine order.

"I now look forward to a glorious future. I live in the joyous expectancy of the best. All of the wonderful God-like thoughts I am thinking now, this day, sink down into the subconscious mind as into a tomb. I know that when their time is ready, they will come forth as harmony, health, peace, conditions, experiences and events.

"I now pass over from fear and lack to freedom in God and the abundant life. The God-man is risen in me. Behold! I make all things new!"

CHAPTER 7

Thought Patterns Are Creative

The faculty of imagination, in the estimate of masses of the world population, and even among those who are presumed to be highly educated, has been greatly undervalued. With many, imagination has been degraded to a lower level among their intellectual powers. Nevertheless, remember that imagination is really one of the highest and most important powers within you.

Imagination is the formative power of your mind. It has creative potency. God created the universe and the galaxies of space by imagining Himself to be all of these things, and He became what He imagined Himself to be. God had to image man for man to appear.

Consider fiction writers for a moment and realize that all of the wonderful scenes they create are products of a lively imagination. Fiction, in the etymological sense, is that which the imagination creates. Poetry is a mental creation. The imagination is the image-making faculty, or that which forms an idea which is projected on the screen of space.

The imagination is the foremost faculty of man. It is

112

a spiritual force and a creative power. The very fact that a man imagines himself to be sick is a proof that he is so, for the disease is only the effect of the misuse and the abnormal action of this creative power. If we could trace the mental history of every ailment or disease in individuals, we would undoubtedly discover the power of misdirected imagination.

You can use any power two ways. Be sure to use disciplined, controlled, directed imagination based on universal principles and eternal verities. Imagine what is lovely, noble, dignified and God-like. Imagination combined with faith works wonders in effecting healings of all manner of diseases. In these two spiritual powers—namely, imagination and faith—we have the most important of all creative devices.

He Ministered to a Mind Diseased

The late Carrick Cook, who was a minister in San Francisco for many years and an associate of the late Ernest Holmes, founder of the Science of Mind in Los Angeles, once told me about a black woman who was a remarkable healer. It seems that someone had sold her a bone relic presumed to be that of a saint, and she had been convinced that when people came to her for a healing, if they would only touch that bone, they would be healed of whatever infirmity they had.

Great numbers were truly healed, but in the words of Carrick Cook, it was actually the bone of a dog. The patients who had come to her believed what she said, and their faith and imagination did the rest. Carrick

Cook said a medical doctor who had examined the bone explained to her that it was part of the foot of a dog.

This shows you the power of faith and imagination, which resurrected the healing power within those who accepted what the practitioner had said. This, of course, was blind faith, as they had no understanding of how or why they were healed. True faith is the union of your conscious and subconscious mind, scientifically directed.

The most potent forces of nature act silently, with no noise. Your thoughts have power over your body. Your thoughts may be morbific, a type which generates disease; or your thoughts may be wholesome, constructive and promotive of health. The state of thinking and feeling is the cause of the bodily condition.

Thoughts and ideas represent the underlying reality of all outward and visible objects. As you look out at the world, everything you see, such as the starry heavens, the mountains, seas, lakes, trees, etc., are the thoughts of God. By studying nature, we communicate with the Infinite, in the same way as we do with the ideas of an author by reading the words of his book.

Let Us Look at the Power of Thoughts

Whatever a man consciously creates or invents is always first a thought in his mind, an idea clearly formulated in his mind, before it is shaped into an objective, or external thing. For example, the house you live in, the automobile you drive or the airplane in which you fly first exists in the mind of man. The picture is in the mind of the painter, and the wonderful statue you admire was first an idea in the mind of the sculptor.

Plato taught that everything exists in ideas or thought images in the mind before it can have external realization. There are false ideas and true ones, a right and a wrong way of thinking. A false or fallacious idea can manifest itself in the body as disease. Fulton's idea became manifested as a steamboat and Morse's idea into a telegraph. A factory or large department store is the thought of an entrepreneur condensed into objective manifestation.

People are waking up to the influence of ideas, imagination, faith and feeling over the corporeal condition and all the physiological functions of your being.

Where Are the Enemies?

Frequently I receive letters from men and women who ask, "How can I forgive or love those who rape, murder, steal, plunder, rob, mistreat their children and in some cases murder them?" They go on and talk about Iranians who hold Americans in hostage and treat them so cruelly.

In the Bible it says: . . . *Love your enemies, bless them that curse you, do good to them that hate you, and pray for them which despitefully use you, and per-secute you* (Matthew 5:44). Many people misinterpret and misunderstand the real meaning of "love your enemies." You are also told that the enemies are of your own household (mind). If the thoughts in your mind are hateful, resentful, angry and full of rancor and bitterness, you are emotionally disturbed. Your health suffers, perhaps bringing on disease, such as ulcers, high blood pressure, failure in business and poor human relations.

Why He Did Not Prosper

Some time ago a brilliant businessman who had achieved great success in his field of expression said that his business was dropping off, his clerks were stealing, and many of his customers had gone elsewhere.

The reason was that he was involved in a marital problem, a bitterly contested divorce. He hated his wife, and his mind was polluted with anger, suppressed rage and fear. The enemies were created by himself.

I explained to him that he was the only thinker in his world and that he was responsible for the way he was thinking about his wife. He began to see clearly that it is not what happens to him but his reaction to it—the way he thinks about it—that makes the difference between success and failure, or health and sickness.

Accordingly, he practiced the law of substitution. He supplanted his negative thoughts with constructive thoughts and began to claim that there was a Divine, harmonious solution to his legal problem and that Divine justice would reign supreme.

He discovered that the real enemies had been his own thoughts, created by him; so he practiced right thought, right feeling and right action. A simple prayer he used was, "God thinks, speaks and acts through me. God loves me and cares for me." When fear or hateful thoughts came to his mind, he immediately affirmed, "God's love fills my soul." Thus, he healed himself and his business prospered.

Psychosomatic Medicine

The word *psychosomatic* comes from two Greek words, *psyche,* meaning mind, and *soma,* meaning the body, indicating that nothing happens in the body unless the equivalent is first in your mind. Dr. Frank Varese in Laguna Hills is an outstanding medical doctor, and he frequently lectures on the relation between mind and body in disease. He, together with other doctors practicing holistic medicine, stresses the relationship between physical disorders and the various diseases and the tangled and destructive emotions of their patients.

Oncologists, who specialize in the treatment of cancer, point out that there is usually a pattern of deep-seated resentment, hostility and frustration, and an unwillingness to forgive, coupled with self-condemnation and a deep sense of guilt behind cancer patients. The disease is the outpicturing of the thought patterns

117

of the patient. Dr. Varese is very successful in bringing about a state of healthy-mindedness in his patients.

You can readily see the wisdom of loving your enemies when you understand that the enemies are created by yourself and are, in reality, a movement of your own mind. Therefore, when you supplant your negative thoughts with God-like thoughts based on eternal verities, the negative thoughts are changed into constructive energy, which bless and heal you.

The Two Sisters

A pair of twin sisters were married at the same time and were apparently very much in love with their husbands. After a few years, however, the two husbands deserted them and went to foreign countries, leaving no explanation and making no provision for rearing the child born to each one of the sisters.

One of the sisters, who had studied the science of mind, went back to nursing, maintaining her poise, equilibrium and balance. She continued to take her beauty treatments and her swimming and golf exercises and maintained her inner peace. She continued to dwell on the great truths contained in *Songs of God.** She never lost her composure. Like Joseph of old, she maintained that only good could come out of this experience. She quickly got a divorce and the

---

*See *Songs of God* by Dr. Joseph Murphy, DeVorss and Company, Inc., Marina del Rey, California, 1979.

pediatrician who had been attending to her young daughter proposed to her and they were married.

The other sister expressed her intense hatred toward her ex-husband, wishing for him all sorts of negative experiences. She was seething with rage and hostility and got an acute case of arthritis and had to be confined to a hospital.

Both sisters had had the same experience; the difference was not in what had happened to them but in their thoughts and their reactions to the experience.

You know where the enemy is. You cannot afford resentment, hatred, hostility or emotional stress because these emotions rob you of discernment, vitality, peace of mind and health, leaving you a physical and mental wreck. Truly, it pays dividends to love your enemies.

Dominion of the Mind

There is no part of the body that is not under the dominion of the mind and that cannot be influenced by an intelligent voluntary action. I knew a man in India who could suspend the pulsation of his heart at will. This capacity is well known in research circles today.

There were other teachers at the Ashram who could perspire at will. Others were able to contract or dilate the pupils of the eyes as they wished. They said that all they had to do was to think of a very dark place and the pupils of the eyes would dilate. When they thought of a very bright spot the pupils of the eyes would con-tract. For example, if you think of something sour, such as lemon juice, it affects your salivary glands and causes your mouth to water.

Thus, an idea, a thought, an imagination, may act as a medicine or as a poison. *For as he thinketh in his heart, so is he.* . . (Proverbs 23:7). This is one of the wisest things Solomon ever said. In your subconscious mind reside all the active, vital powers. Given a certain mental state, a corresponding bodily condition follows with the unerring certainty of the law of cause and effect. There is a power in thought over all the organs of our body that is not recognized by the masses.

To live truly means to think truly and to discern the truth. It is important to bear in mind that imagination is a mode of thought, and every idea in the mind tends by its inherent nature to an actuality in the body. The only living force of the body is the mind.

Remember a simple truth: It is your thought, created by yourself, that is the real enemy. Come to a point of decision regarding these enemies in your mind and cast them out. Consume them and burn them up with the fire of Divine love. It is foolish to assume that loving your enemies means to invite felons, rapists, murderers and dope fiends into your home and enter-tain them, putting your arms around them and telling them how much you love them. That is absurd.

You understand why they act the way they do. They are under the compulsion of negative, destructive and irrational emotions. You understand that they are full of self-hatred and are projecting that on to others. You look upon them with a degree of comprehension and tolerance. You do not under any circumstances condone their crimes, but you understand the malignant forces operating in their minds. Furthermore, you realize that justice and punishment will prevail.

The murderers, rapists, etc., should be incarcerated so that society may be protected. Some do-gooders who have little or no understanding of wisdom and who are on the parole boards, oftentimes release these hardened criminals to prey again on society. One such criminal freely admitted to me that he pretended to be religious and said that he was converted and born again, so they released him. That is not love. There is no love without wisdom and no wisdom without love.

Learn the Mental and Spiritual Laws of Life

More importantly, to love your enemies means to banish from your mind your fears, hates, jealousies, angers and resentments, all of which are self-created, for these are your real enemies. If these negative emotions dominate and control your mind, you can be absolutely sure to experience the result in your body, your home, your business and your relationship with others. This is the mental and spiritual law operating in all men and women throughout the world, regardless of their religious affiliations and nominal beliefs. Hunters tell us that animals pick up the scent of fear and will attack you.

In consultation with a woman today as I write this

chapter, she admitted that she had lived in constant fear that her home would be robbed. While she was at church one Sunday, thieves pulled a truck up in front of her house and carried away all the expensive furnishings in her home. They cleaned her out.

Her constant fear, morning, noon and night, had been the real thief, and her subconscious had brought it to pass. The law is impersonal and no respecter of persons. She is now using the great Psalm of protection, which is the 91st Psalm,* and will build up an immunity to all harm.

Let all the thoughts in your mind be harmonious, peaceful, loving and based on faith in God and the goodness of God in the land of the living. Let your trust and reliance be in God, the Source of all blessings. When your thoughts are God's thoughts, God's power is with your thoughts of good.

"Of the soul the body form doth take, for soul is form and doth the body make."

The Power of Suggestion in Healing

There is an interesting article written by Dr. Warren Evans, who was a student of Phineas Parkhurst Quimby about 1850. He quotes an historical event: At the siege of Buda in 1625, when the garrison was on the point of surrendering, in consequence of the

---

*See *Songs of God* by Dr. Joseph Murphy. DeVorss and Company. Inc.. Marina del Rey. California. 1979.

prevalence of scurvy in an aggravated form, the Prince of Orange caused to be introduced a few bottles of sham medicine as a sovereign remedy and infallible specific for the disease. This, given in drops, produced the most astonishing effects.

Many who had not moved their limbs for months were seen walking in the streets sound, straight and whole; and many who declared that they had been rendered worse by all former remedies recovered in a few days. Of course, you realize it was not the effect of the medicine, which had no therapeutic value whatever. It was their faith and confidence in the remedial value of the drops that effected the amazing therapeutic results.

It would be wonderful if all people became aware of the Infinite Healing Presence within them and then realized that their faith in the response of this Healing Presence would work wonders in their lives. They could use their imagination wisely and knowingly, realizing that as they imagined themselves doing all of the things they would do were they whole, their subconscious would respond.

This would represent a sincere act of faith in God, which is a movement of the mind and heart towards the Infinite Healing Presence Which created us, thus bringing about a vital union and a vivifying conjunction with the Divine Presence which indwells all of us. Wonders would happen when we prayed knowingly and lovingly.

HOW TO USE THE LAWS OF MIND

You Are Here to Grow and Expand

Read the first Psalm. It is a beautiful drama setting forth how man can release the Divinity within him and express himself at his highest level. *And he shall be like a tree planted by the rivers of water, that bringeth forth his fruit in his season; his leaf also shall not wither: and whatsoever he doeth shall prosper* (Psalm 1:3).

You can see the analogy clearly. The tree has its roots in the soil, and there is a subjective wisdom within the tree enabling its roots to suck up and appropriate from the soil all of the chemicals and nutrients necessary for its unfoldment. These roots dig deep into the soil and extract the waters of life for the tree.

Likewise, you are rooted in the Life-Principle, and as you turn to that Infinite Spirit within you and unite mentally and spiritually with the Living Spirit, you will be refreshed, revitalized, regenerated and inspired from On High. The Tree of Life is within you, and the fruits of that tree are love, joy, peace, harmony, guidance, right action and illumination. You can draw out of the depths of yourself everything you need to lead a full and happy life.

The Word Made Flesh

In the beginning was the Word, and the Word was with God, and the Word was God (John 1:1). A word is a thought expressed, and it is creative. It is the only immaterial power we know. Your thought is God in the sense that it is a creative power at the level of the individual mind. It is not God in the sense of Universal Mind and Infinite Spirit.

The word of God which people speak of represents the truth of God, which is the same yesterday, today and forever. The Bible says: . . . *Say in a word, and my servant shall be healed* (Luke 7:7).

When you pray for another, you claim that what is true of God is also true of the sick person. Turn to the Indwelling Presence and Power (God) and remind yourself of absolute peace, absolute harmony, beauty, boundless love and limitless power. Cease dwelling on symptoms, organs, or any part of the body. Feel and know that there is only one Healing Presence and Power; quietly and lovingly affirm the uplifting, healing, strengthening power of the Infinite Healing Presence flowing through the person you are praying for, making him whole and perfect. Know and feel that the harmony, beauty, wholeness and love of God are manifesting in the other. Get a clear realization of this; then you will be sending the word which heals.

Remove the Mental Blocks

I have talked to a great number of young men and women. Many of them have charm, intelligence, excellent educations and a sense of humor, but they do not believe in themselves. They are down on themselves, so to speak. The usual story is that they were told when they were young that they were stupid, dumb, awkward and ungainly; and they were handicapped by these preconceptions of inferiority and weakness. They seemed to be living in an illusion that is not real.

I tell the men to look into the mirror in the morning and for about five minutes affirm out loud, with feeling: "I AM a son of the Living God. I exalt God in the midst of me. I can do all things through the God Power which strengtheneth me." I urge them to keep it up regularly and, when prone to criticize or find fault with themselves, to affirm at once, "I exalt God in the midst of me." This neutralizes the negative thought, and the fear thought is changed into constructive energy.

I teach the young women to use the mirror treatment also, affirming: "I AM a daughter of the Infinite. I AM a child of Eternity. God is my Father, and God loves me and cares for me." Whenever they are prone to condemn or demote themselves, they will affirm immediately: "God loves me and He careth for me."

Gradually, all of the negative patterns implanted in childhood disappear and are completely wiped out. Their minds had become the victims of negative suggestions which were accepted by them when very young, as their minds were impressionable and malleable. They did not have the wisdom or understanding to reject the negative suggestions at that time. Many parents thoughtlessly, carelessly and perhaps

126

ignorantly, call the young boy a liar or dumb; and they tend to make him one when they keep repeating it. The boy begins to accept the suggestion and his subconscious, being the seat of habit and compulsive in nature, expresses his belief.

The Old Proverb Says It Well

"Give a dog a bad name and hang him." There is a certain degree of truth in that old proverb. A secretary to the president of a company said to me that the other girls in the office were spreading all manner of lies about her, accusing her of all manner of sexual deviations—a sort of character assassination generating a lot of hostility and ill will in the office.

I suggested to her that she pay no attention to the lies propagated by the girls in the office, since their gossip and suggestions had no power to create the things they suggested, and that she had the power to reject them and ignore them. She began dwelling on the inner meaning of the 91st Psalm* and practiced the great truths during each day. She had the courage and the fortitude to rely on the Infinite Presence within her. They quickly saw that their accusations and negative whisperings had no effect on her.

The sequel was interesting: Those who were spreading the false accusations were transferred, and the

---

*See *Songs of God* by Dr. Joseph Murphy, DeVorss and Company, Inc., Marina del Rey, California, 1979.

secretary announced to the remaining girls that she was marrying the president of the organization.

This is the prayer she used frequently: *"God is all there is. One with God is a majority. If God be for me who can be against me?* (Romans 8:31). I know and believe God is the Living Spirit Almighty—the Ever-Living One, the All-Wise One—and there is no power to challenge God. I know and accept completely that when my thoughts are God's thoughts, God's power is with my thoughts of good. I know I cannot receive what I cannot give, and I give out thoughts of love, peace, light and goodwill to all those around me and to all people everywhere. I am immunized and God-intoxicated and I am always surrounded by the sacred circle of God's love. The whole armor of God surrounds me and enfolds me. I am Divinely guided and directed, and I enter into the joy of living. *In thy presence is fulness of joy; at thy right hand there are pleasures for evermore* (Psalm 16:11)."

CHAPTER 8

Fulfill Your Desires

God is forever seeking expression through you. God speaks to man through desire. If you are sick, you desire health; if poor, you desire wealth; if in prison, you desire freedom; if lost in the jungle, you desire to find your way out and be secure.

The realization of your desire is your savior. Everyone is his own savior, and every man answers his own prayer, because whatever he really believes comes to pass. You have a desire to grow, expand, unfold and realize your heart's desire. You desire to be greater tomorrow than you are today.

If you are a musician you don't want to be a mediocre musician; you desire to excel so that your music may stir the souls of men and women. Scientists desire to know more of the secrets of the genetic code; other scientists delve into the secrets of the atom. Their desire or hunger for more knowledge of cosmic laws and the secrets of the universe is continuing to bless mankind in countless ways. The urge to express is in everything, everywhere.

Your Innermost Desire

Your real innermost desire is to find your true expression in life where you are doing what you love to do, Divinely happy and Divinely prospered. You may do six things well, but there is one thing you can do better than the six—that is your true place, or true expression.

Your Higher Self knows all your talents and will reveal to you the answer. Affirm, "Infinite Intelligence within me reveals my true place in life and I follow the lead which comes clearly into my conscious, reasoning mind." The lead will come to you. Follow it. You desire to express yourself at your highest level and exercise your faculties at the highest degree, and you desire a marvelous and wonderful income consistent with integrity and honesty.

Desire is Natural and God-Given

Some years ago I was acquainted with a Spanish girl who was working in a department store. She told me in consultation that all she wanted to do with her life was to become a singer. She had a wonderful, trained voice. She tried to get a contract to sing on television, radio and night clubs but met repeatedly with rejection. She was very frustrated and all bottled up, in a manner of speaking.

She understood that by repressing her desire to sing and go forward to new areas of living brought about ulcers in her system. So she changed her attitude, and her changed attitude changed everything. She turned within to her Higher Self and affirmed: "Infinite Spirit gave me this desire to sing and opens up the way for my perfect expression in Divine law and order." She made sure that she did not subsequently deny what she affirmed.

Shortly after her prayer process, she was invited to sing at a Spanish club, and a new career opened up for her almost immediately with a greater income, greater prestige, and, above all, she was expressing her real talent to the world.

Self-Preservation

Self-preservation is the first law of life, which means that the first desire of life is to preserve itself and to expand along all lines. Your desire to be, to do, to have and to express yourself in a wonderful way, living life to the fullest, is a powerful urge within you.

There is the sex desire planted in you for the continuance of the race. Sex is a love act and must never be used to inflict harm or guilt on another. It must be based on mutual love, freedom and respect. You can give all of your desires healthful expression.

Desire Is the Gift of God

Desire is basic in life. Desire is! It is impossible to get rid of desire. If you are hungry, you want food; if thirsty, you want water. A man asked the electrical wizard, Thomas Edison, "Mr. Edison, what is electricity?" Edison said, "Electricity is. Use it."

You can use the power to bless mankind in countless ways. You can also use it to electrocute someone. You can thus use any power two ways. You never, under any circumstances, should desire another man's job, his wife, his home or anything that is his. To covet or envy another is to attract loss, lack and limitation to yourself. You impoverish yourself along all lines. You are saying to yourself, "He can have these things, but I can't." You are denying your own Divinity. To steal from another mentally is to actually steal from yourself.

The loss can come to you in many ways: loss of health, prestige, promotion, love or money. The way loss comes is past finding out. You do not want the other fellow's position: You really want a position like it, giving you the same privileges, emoluments, salary and perquisites.

Infinite Intelligence can open a new door of expression for you if you call upon it. You will get an answer.

Suppression of Desire

In India and other places in the East students are taught to suppress their desires. This is foolish and has disastrous consequences. One woman said to me that she wanted to reach the place where she did not want anything, and then she would be free. However, she was the most frustrated, neurotic woman I have ever met in any Ashram.

FULFILL YOUR DESIRES

I asked her: "Don't you desire a cup of coffee in the morning? If you are a musician, don't you desire to play music and lift others up? If you are a medical doctor, don't you desire to alleviate pain and suffering? If you are a farmer, don't you desire to plant and harvest and have food for your children?"

His Desire Was to Go to College

A young man was stealing money from his employer and was caught and discharged. He said to me later, by way of explanation, that he stole because he wanted to go to college. He had misdirected his desire. There was nothing wrong with the desire to go to college. I explained to him that God, who gave him the desire, does not mock him and that he has the unqualified capacity to go to the God-Presence within and claim his good. I added that God, being the Source of everything in the world, would somehow open up the way for him to complete his college course.

I gave him a simple prayer, as follows: "God is the Source of my supply, and God's wealth is circulating in my life. There is always a Divine surplus. God opens up the way for me to enter college in Divine order."

I explained to him that his desire was good but that he had misdirected it and misused the law of mind. You do not steal, rob or injure another in order to get ahead. To do so is to attract all manner of loss and limitation to yourself. The mere fact that you steal indicates you are in a mood of lack, followed by a sense of guilt, all of which have destructive consequences.

So he used the law constructively based on the above prayer, and the way opened up for him. He won a scholarship and found the Source of all blessings.

Reason Things Out

If you did not desire, you would not make any choices. However, you are a choosing, volitional being. If you made no choices, you would not grow. You would not do anything. In everyday language, you would not exist. If you did not desire, nothing would rouse your interest. You would be dead to love, to peace, to laughter and to motivation. You would shrivel up spiritually, emotionally and physically. Actually, you would be a nonentity.

Trying to suppress or eradicate desire is a sort of spiritual suicide. Welcome the desires for health, happiness, peace, joy and true expression. You are here to express all the qualities, attributes and potencies of God. You are here to reveal more and more of your Divinity every day. You are here to contribute to humanity, to put your shoulder to the wheel and to make the world a better place to live in. You are here to glorify God and enjoy Him forever.

There Is an Answer

Realize that desire is the motivating force behind all progress and advancement in science, art, industry and in all phases of life. It is the moving principle behind all of your achievements. There is an answer for every true desire of the heart. There is a right way

FULFILL YOUR DESIRES

to fulfill your soul's sincere desire. You could not
desire unless the answer to the desire existed. Realize
that Infinite Spirit which gave you the desire will reveal
to you the perfect plan for its unfoldment in Divine law
and order.

Paul said, *For it is God which worketh in you both
to will and to do of his good pleasure* (Philippians
2:13). You desire to excel and grow in wisdom. This
desire is of God, the Life Principle, working in and
through you, urging you to climb the ladder of life
and express yourself at higher levels. Do not repress
desire. To do so is to repress the Life Principle, Itself.
It is foolish to refuse to breathe air or drink water,
since death would quickly follow.

The Golden Rule

Every great religion down through countless ages
has taught the Golden Rule, which means, in a simple
way, that you wish health, happiness, peace, prosperity and all the blessings of life for all people everywhere. You are here to serve and give of your talents
and abilities to the world. The joy is in serving. As
you serve others nobly, generously and lovingly, your
good will return to you a thousandfold; furthermore,
you will receive honor, recognition and wonderful
financial rewards for work well done.

Find a need in your location and fill it. The world
will richly reward you. Wherever you are, and no
matter what kind of work you are engaged in, you can
help others to help themselves. You can always give a

transfusion of faith and confidence to all those around you. You can give joy and gladness and exalt the Divinity in all of your co-workers, as well as all people everywhere. This attitude of mind will pay fabulous dividends.

She Found a Need

Speaking in the St. Louis Church of Religious Science recently, a girl from Peru told me that she had come to St. Louis three years ago and was working as a translator in an office. She heard men and women frequently say that it would be wonderful to have a good Spanish restaurant nearby. Since she had had experience as a cook in Lima, Peru, she told some of the men that she could operate a restaurant and fill this need. Two men in the organization decided to back her financially, and today she is a wonderful success.

Mental and spiritual food is just as necessary as physical food. Food for the body is a prerequisite, as it is very difficult to convey the great truths of life to a hungry man. God's ideas enthroned in your mind and Divine inspiration are just as essential as bread and meat. Furthermore, you have to love and be loved if you want to live life nobly.

You Are Needed

Every person wants to feel needed and wanted, and desires to achieve his true place in life. In other

136

words, he wants his riches in life and all the necessary money to do what he wants to do when he wants to do it. Money is a symbol of freedom, luxury, refinement, abundance and security.

Look to the Source of all blessings and affirm from an Infinite standpoint: "God's wealth, spiritual, mental, material and financial, is circulating in my life and there is always a Divine surplus." The Infinite Intelligence within you will respond according to the universal law of action and reaction.

Each person is unique and wants to express himself at his highest level. To be successful in the art of living, contribute to the well-being and fulfillment of other people's desires and hopes. Then you will be prospered. Recall the old Hindu maxim, "Help thy brother's boat across and, lo, thine own hath reached the shore." The most worthwhile and truly successful person is the one who continuously aids and assists other people to achieve their hearts' desires.

The Two Brothers

Two brothers went into business together and were doing fairly well for several years. Recently, they started to play the futures market and the commodity market and ended up losing everything, including all their business and savings. Actually, they owed $50,000, which they were unable to pay, and they went bankrupt.

I talked with one brother, who had a very good

attitude. He said, "I have lost money. I will make it again and I will go into business again. I have learned a good lesson, which will ultimately pay me dividends. I have not lost my faith, my confidence or my ability to rise and grow. I have much to offer and I am going to be a tremendous success again."

He went to work for a brokerage firm and, due to his large number of friends, he had no trouble acquiring new accounts for his employers.

He also told me about his brother, whom he had tried to get to change his attitude. It seems that his brother felt humiliated and disgraced because he had lost everything. He started telling everyone he met about his losses and monotonously repeated the old refrain that it was his broker's fault, seeking justification for his own wrong decisions and errors. His friends began to shun him and his health was adversely affected by his gloom and despondency. He refused counselling and went on welfare.

Here you have two brothers who experienced the same loss. One reacted constructively and the other reacted negatively and with a complete sense of futility. It is not what happens to us individually that matters so much; it is our thought about it, our reaction, which can be constructive or negative. One brother used his imagination wisely, rebuilding in his mind a new pattern, seeing future possibilities, using the wings of faith and imagination for rebuilding a better life. He discovered that success and wealth were in his own mind.

Creative Imagination

Creative imagination is a marvelous spiritual quality. All of the great discoveries and inventions in science, art and industry came forth from men with disciplined imaginations. When the whole world said, "It can't be done," men with imagination said, "It is done."

Primitive man living in caves was at the mercy of wild beasts, but a budding imagination enabled him to fashion certain clubs, stones and other crude instruments which could kill the beasts which attacked him. The tremendous odds against primitive man forced him to imagine and create all kinds of crude weapons to protect himself. He created fire to warm him and cook his food and eventually discovered the wheel, which has blessed mankind in countless ways. The dimensions of imagination are, indeed, boundless, infinite and limitless.

She Wanted a Home

A widow with a son ten years old wanted a home near her work in the Newport area. She imagined that she was in the home arranging the furniture and showing the yard to her boy. In her imagination, she saw the type of rooms she wanted, including a fireplace. In her imagination she was often showing the house to her close friends. She acted as though she had the home, knowing that, as the night follows the day, she would eventually have it. All of this was based on her belief that . . . *What things soever ye desire, when ye pray, believe that ye receive them, and ye shall have them* (Mark 11:24).

A few months went by and a young man in the office where she worked proposed to her. They got married and the home he had was a replica of what she had been imagining and living in mentally for the previous two months. A home is a thought-image in your mind.

There Is an Easy Way

There are many people who think the way to get ahead is to brush others aside, step over them, push, scramble, out-smart and out-do the other. All of this is absolutely false. You may get ahead that way in a materialistic sense for a time, but the reaction can bring upon you serious penalties in tensions, conflicts, a sense of guilt, and ills of the body as well as various other losses.

To hurt another is to hurt yourself and attract loss, lack, limitation and impoverishment to yourself. To envy others and seek to "undermine" them will cause you to find dross at the end, not gold.

Develop a vivid imagination, backed by faith in God. You will then move onward and upward and accomplish great things. Mussolini, Stalin, Hitler and others used the creative power of imagination to destroy others. In doing so, they succeeded in destroying themselves.

FULFILL YOUR DESIRES

There Is a Light Within You

Years ago I read the words uttered by the late King George of England. He quoted the poet, who had said, "I said to the man who stood at the Gate of the Year, 'Give me a light that I may tread safely into the Unknown.' And he replied, 'Go out into the darkness and put your hand into the hand of God. That shall be to you better than a light and safer than a known way.'"

The light referred to is the Supreme Intelligence within you that knows all and sees all. As you turn to this Indwelling Light, It will turn to you and lead you to green pastures and still waters.

His Mental Picture of His Daughter

A physician's daughter was in the hospital, gravely ill. She was receiving expert medical care but was not responding as she should, according to medical findings.

I suggested to the doctor, her father, that he quiet his mind frequently during the day and imagine the love-light in his daughter's eyes as he talked to her. She embraced him in his imagination with deep affection and kept saying to him, "Daddy, I am completely well. Take me home." He kept running this movie in his mind; and one of his confreres, who was attending his child, phoned him to say, "There has been a remarkable change and drop in temperature in

141

your daughter. She is normal in every way. You can take her home."

Her father truly experienced what formerly he imagined he was hearing and experiencing. This was the constructive use of imagination and the natural response of Life.

You Are Always Imagining

All men and women possess the faculty of imagination. It is the primal faculty within us. Imagine what is lovely and of good report. If your mother is in the hospital, imagine instead that she is at home, doing all of the things she would normally do were she whole. Hear her tell you about the miraculous healing she has had. Make it all real and vivid and rejoice in the reality of it. You will find that she will confirm your conviction of her.

The Misuse of Imagination

Many people are constantly reading murder stories; looking at horror movies; and dwelling upon the violence, viciousness and depravity of murderers, rapists and pornographers. Ofttimes these people have frightful nightmares at night.

When you find so-called gentle people absorbed in these murder mysteries and sordid movies, these experiences give them a sort of vicarious release of their inner hostility, suppressed rage and anger. This vicarious slaughter taking place in their minds brings

about all manner of inner conflicts and physical disorders. These emotions are highly destructive.

Instead, get a vision of loveliness that delights you
and you will have no room in your mind for such
vicarious experiences in these morbid, gruesome and
depraved external movies.

Why the Speaker Failed

A young man, a recent graduate from the ministerial school, experienced what he called "stage fright."
He was asked to substitute for another minister on a
Sunday morning. He told me that he had a mental
picture of defeat, failure and humiliation. He stut-
tered, became tongue-tied at times, began to perspire
and even forgot what he wanted to say. These pic-
tures were created by himself. The audience, however,
was not hostile, but friendly.

He reversed the procedure and began to realize that
the Spirit in him was talking to the Spirit in all of the
members of the congregation. He began to imagine a
circle of light and love enfolding the audience. He
affirmed: "God thinks, speaks and acts through me
and I radiate love, peace and goodwill to them." He
imagined them smiling. In his mind he heard many of
them say, "That was a wonderful sermon." He imagined the members of the board congratulating him.

He kept this up the following week. The following
Sunday he was warmly received and gave a splendid
talk. He had used his imagination wisely.

HOW TO USE THE LAWS OF MIND

An Old Mystic Legend

The ancient Bible writers wrote in allegories, fables, myths, parables and fiction in order to portray great psychological and spiritual truths. I read the following story years ago, and I will condense it into everyday language.

The old legend said that the gods had a secret conclave in Heaven and decided that the hidden wisdom of the ages should be given to man so he would for the first time know that the God which created all things and was all-powerful and all-wise was within himself, the very Reality of him. One of the younger gods pleaded with his elders that he be selected to impart and convey this wonderful message to mankind. He added that he did not care what the trials, difficulties and tribulations might be—but that he would meet them and overcome. The other gods voted on it, and they gave him permission to take the priceless "Jewel of Truth" to mankind.

He was overjoyed and ecstatic over this opportunity. On reaching the planet earth, he stumbled and the "Jewel of Truth" was broken and scattered into thousands and thousands of particles all over the earth. This caused confusion on the planet earth because forever after, when men found particles of this Jewel, each one fancied that he alone had found the Truth.

The above story is about the essence of the old legend. Today, all over the world, we have countless

144

creeds, dogmas, ceremonies, rituals and sectarian groups, each proclaiming that they have the Truth. No one has a monopoly on Truth. God is the Truth— the same yesterday, today and forever. You cannot put a label on the Truth.

The ancients said, "When you name It, you cannot find It, and when you find It, you cannot name It." The root of the word religion is "to bind." What binds you is your real religion. Your dominant idea about God is your religion. Millions throughout the world are governed by fear; others are governed by rank superstition.

Your dominant idea or conviction controls all lesser thoughts, ideas and opinions. True religion is to be bound back to God. Enthrone a God of love in your mind and let God's love govern all of your thoughts, feelings and actions. Let God be your guide, your counsellor, your troubleshooter and wayshower. Think, speak and act from the Divine Center within you and then you will find that His name is Wonderful. Having God as your boss and your guide, you will find that all your ways are pleasantness and all your paths are peace.

CHAPTER 9

The Explanation Is the Cure

Dr. Phineas Quimby, who started teaching and healing in Maine in 1847, often used the term, "The explanation is the cure." By this Dr. Quimby meant that his explanation as to why the patient had the particular disease was a penetrating truth aiding the sick person to change his mind and keep it changed.

The cure was wrought by his insight. When the patient grasped his explanation, the cure was immediate insofar as the inner life was concerned.

Last year I said to a girl in a convent which I visited in England, who had suddenly lost her voice: "You feel guilty. You would like to speak out about it, but you feel you should not and your subconscious has responded accordingly." She nodded her head, attesting to the truth of what I had said. She forthwith came to a decision to speak to the Sister Superior of the convent and her voice came back immediately. The explanation was the cure in that instance.

Dr. Quimby very suddenly and convincingly spoke to some of his patients that illuminating word which brought far-reaching results affecting the health, religion and mode of life of his patients. Quimby was clairvoyant. He said the test of clairvoyance is the ability to read a letter in the pocket of another person, which that person had not yet read.

Ulcerated Thoughts

Some time ago, in consultation, a man said to me that he was on a milk diet and was taking medicine for his ulcers. Casually, I mentioned that ulcers are generally due to worry, fear, anxiety, deep-seated resentment, stress and strain. He admitted that this statement was absolutely true.

The next step was to teach him that if these habitual thoughts had created his ulcers, he could reverse his thought life and instead contemplate regularly thoughts of peace, harmony, right action, love, goodwill, wholeness and vitality. All he had to do was to make a habit of constructive spiritual thinking. He had been attributing his ulcers to heredity, diet and other factors.

I gave him the following patterns of prayer to be spoken out loud three times in the morning, three times in the afternoon and three times at night prior to sleep: *"The Lord is my light and my salvation; whom shall I fear? the Lord is the strength of my life; of whom shall I be afraid?* (Psalms 27:1). I have a new, strong conviction of God's Presence which holds me spellbound, entranced and unmoved, and I feel serene, confident, and unafraid. I know there is nothing to fear—nothing to draw away from, for God is all there is and everywhere present. In Him I live, move and have my being, so I have no fear. God's envelope of love surrounds me and His golden river of peace flows through me; all is well. I am not afraid of people, conditions, events or circumstances, for God is with me. Faith in God fills my soul, and I have no fear. I dwell in the Presence of God now and forevermore, and no fear can touch me. I am not afraid of the future, for God is with me. He is my dwelling place, and I am surrounded with the whole armor of God. God created me and He sustains me. God's wisdom leads and guides me; so I cannot err. I know in my heart the great truth, 'Closer is He than breathing, nearer than hands and feet.' "

He followed this procedure regularly, and after a reasonable period of time his doctor, who was much surprised, pronounced him healed. The explanation was the cure. The clarifying words of truth work wonders when accepted by the mind of the sick or confused person.

He Saw that He Was Foolish

A businessman frankly admitted to me recently that he was wishing failure for a competitor across the street from him. The reason he gave was that the competitor was underselling him. His prices for the same merchandise were much lower.

THE EXPLANATION IS THE CURE

I explained to him that his attitude was very foolish, because what he was wishing for the other he was at the same time wishing for himself. He was the only thinker in his world, and, because his thoughts are creative, he was attracting lack, loss and limitation and was actually impoverishing himself.

He saw the point immediately. His competitor obviously believed in success, prosperity and expansion and, therefore, could not receive his negative thoughts of failure. He detected his folly and grasped immediately the cause of his slow business. He quickly dropped his negative thinking and prayed for the prosperity and success of his competitor. Then he found that he prospered, also.

To bless the other is to bless yourself. Prayer always prospers. There is an old saying: "The ship that comes home to your brother also comes home to you." The explanation was the cure.

The Affair Was Over at Once

A young secretary told me that she was infatuated with one of the engineers in her office. She was, as she said, "madly in love with him." She had been praying for guidance and right action in all of her undertakings, using the 91st Psalm* night and morning.

Suddenly one morning a flash came into her mind to look at his file in the personnel cabinet, and she

*See *Songs of God* by Dr. Joseph Murphy, DeVorss and Company, Inc., Marina del Rey, California, 1979.

discovered that he was already married and had two small children. She realized that she had been duped with promises of marriage, a new home, etc. She realized her predicament and the "affair" was over at once. Nothing is so swift in its effect as truth. Her Higher Self had given her the answer.

Spontaneous Healing

While lecturing in Vienna, Austria, some months ago, I had a very interesting talk with a business woman. She said that about ten years previously she had been bedridden, a fire had broken out in the house and there was no one at hand to help. She had arisen from the bed and dragged herself down four flights of stairs to a place of safety, suffering no relapse.

All she had said in the way of prayer when the conflagration had started was, "God help me." The Power responded. The Infinite Healing Presence and Power was always there, but she had never used it until the fire broke out, compelling her to call upon the Divine Presence. Spirit, or God, cannot be paralyzed.

There are many instances in the annals of medicine where, in cases of shock, fire and emergencies, cripples walk and run. Awareness of the Healing Presence within is necessary. It will then no longer be necessary to shock people into activity.

THE EXPLANATION IS THE CURE

They Were Paralyzed for 16 Years

Dr. Evelyn Fleet of London told me that when she was doing street duty in London during the Second World War, a bomb had hit the wing of one of the hospitals there and that fifteen hopeless paralytics, who had been bedridden for as long as sixteen years, had rushed down the stairs and out into the street. One of them had said, "Oh, I should not be walking. I'm paralyzed." She immediately relapsed, but the other fourteen had been completely healed. These had been instantaneous healings.

Many people throughout the world could be cured quickly if they really wished to be. Great numbers avoid the effort and have concealed motives and intentions. In other words, there are many people who do not want to be healed. There are marvelous help and unbounded infinite resources available to all those who turn in confidence and faith to the Infinite Healing Presence in each of us.

Self-Healing

Self-healing means the awakening in our mind of the truth which sets us free, the dawning in us of the healing power of God, which restores and responds when we call upon it. To unite with that power, declare boldly: "I AM Spirit and have Infinite Life to draw upon now." You will then turn the tide.

Remember also that the vast majority of sick people get well without any help from anybody, and doctors know that. The tendency of life is to heal and restore. Most of our fears are borrowed. They have little basis in fact.

Expectant Attention

It is generally recognized that in order for the therapist's suggestion to take effect in the mind of the percipient, there must be predisposing conditions, such as faith and expectancy. The percipient's favorable and receptive attitude is, in reality, self-suggestion. This auto-suggestion explains many of the wonderful results occurring at sacred shrines where so-called miracles of healing have taken place.

The Value of Laughter

The following article appeared in the San Jose *Mercury* on Sunday, October 7, 1979, by Sandy Rovner of *The Washington Post:*

"Coming 'Unglued' Put Him Together Again"

Norman Cousins is teaching laughter at UCLA Medical School.

Sure, you say, Guffaw 101.

Actually, that's not too wrong.

Bellylaughs made him what he is today, and he'll be the first to tell you.

Until a few years ago he was just your

everyday American literary giant, 40 or so years editor of the Saturday Review of Literature, critic, philosopher, spokesman for international cooperation.

And, oh yes, perpetrator of spoofs (that's the word he likes) in the pages of SRL on (but not limited to) April Fool's Day. Unobtrusive ones, of course, like the Ninas in the Hershfelds: If you didn't know to look for them you'd likely never notice.

Then he got sick. So sick that the doctors all but gave up. All they knew was that he had a degenerative collagen illness. Collagen is the body's glue that holds the cells together. Cousins was, as he puts it, literally 'coming unstuck.'

Medical science was not helping and he was getting worse. On the basis of his own vast reading and some urgent on-the-spot research, he concluded he should dump the medicine he was on (including aspirin) and try Vitamin C for his illness and laughter for his pain.

Allen Funt ('Candid Camera') with an assist from some old Marx Brothers films, took care of the laughter and a cooperative and sympathetic physician got him fixed up with intravenous ascorbic acid.

Now, the most surprising thing about it all

is this: Only the occasional nay-sayer suggests that he would have gotten well anyway.

Cousins doesn't admit to surprise at all. He's 'gratified,' he says, that the prestigious New England Journal of Medicine printed his article about his experience, that this summer he has had published two articles in the similarly prestigious Journal of the American Medical Association, that 14 publishers vied for book rights ('Anatomy of an Illness as Perceived by the Patient, W. W. Norton') just out. That he speaks at medical conventions, including those of the AMA. That he is a professor at a medical school.

He believes he's on to something big, and evidently at least a suspicion that indeed he is, is being shared more and more by the medical establishment.

'Any medical student,' says Cousins, 'can give you a horrendous catalogue of all the terrible things that happen to the body under the impact of negative emotions: fear, hate, rage, exasperation, frustration. You learn about constriction of the blood vessels, increase in blood pressure, excess flow of hydrochloric acid, adrenal depletion, indigestion, headaches.

'But we haven't yet sufficiently recognized that the body does not operate only on one

wave length. It just doesn't respond to negative emotions, it responds to the positive emotions. It's impossible to have one without having the other. But the salutary effect is not as
well understood.'

Cousins knows it has to come from within
and it is this concept he is trying to impart to
the medical students he lectures.

'I'm teaching most of those things that bear
on good medical practice that you generally
don't learn in medical school: the concept of
patient responsibility, the art of listening to
people, respect for life, the importance of
compassion, the need to engage to the fullest
the patient's own healing mechanism, the need
to give a patient the understanding to use his
or her own healing mechanism.

'The doctor,' says Cousins, 'does a better
job when the patient takes his or her own end.
This is not just a matter of being obedient. . . .
For a long time the center of gravity of health
care was outside the individual, represented
symbolically by the doctor saying, in effect,
"Come to me and I'll heal you," or the prescription saying in effect, "Take me and
you'll get better."

'You have to recognize that when people are
sick, it's not just that they're attacked by
a bug, but because their lives are out of

155

bounds. And if you want to help them cope with tension, you've got to give them a side of life they enjoy.

'So medicine is incomplete when it attempts to deal only with the effects . . . the trend in medicine, fortunately, is toward increased respect for immunology. And when you talk about fortifying the body's immunological mechanisms, you're not talking about just physical factors, you have to talk about emotional and spiritual factors.'

At UCLA, Cousins is called an Emotional Support Resource.

'Now,' says Cousins, 'laughter is very easily disparaged, just because it seems to be easy. But it tends to be something of a symbol for the plus things in life. It is related to joy, related to optimism, to the will to live. It tends to crystalize an awful lot of things, at least as the most visible expression of good things that happen inside you or to you.

'So while illness is not a laughing matter, perhaps it ought to be. . . .' "

Hypertension

In conversing with a man suffering from acute high blood pressure, I pointed out to him the comment of many medical men, who claim that one of the chief personality characteristics of persons with high blood pressure is resentment. This man had not only chronic high blood pressure but experienced cardiac spasms at times.

This man had been cheated and swindled out of a large sum of money and, as he said, he was seeking vengeance. I explained to him that if he desired a complete healing he must follow the Biblical injunction: . . . *Vengeance is mine; I will repay, saith the Lord* (Romans 12:19). The spiritual meaning of the word *vengeance* in the Bible is to justify, to vindicate. It means victory of truth over error or any negative state. The Truth of Being and the goodness of God are vindicated in our lives when we turn to God and call on Divine love to saturate our whole being.

I suggested that he release completely to God the man who had swindled him, wishing for him harmony and peace and that he claim frequently for himself: "God's peace fills my mind and heart, and God's love saturates my soul."

Through frequent habitation of his mind with these truths, he realized an inner peace and tranquility. Whenever the man who had cheated him came to his mind, he blessed him by affirming, "God's peace fills your soul." As he changed his mind, his physical condition changed and he eventually healed himself.

The Lord is the law of life. If anyone misuses the law, the latter will always even things up, as action and reaction are equal. The tendency of all life is to heal and restore, but we must permit the Life Principle to heal without hindrance.

This man saw the folly of trying to get even with the

other man in hiring someone else to do him bodily harm. He realized all of this brooding was the cause of his malady and that he had brought it all upon himself. He was stealing health, vitality, discernment and peace of mind from himself and impoverishing himself along all lines.

The explanation is the cure, as he perceived that nothing happens by chance. The reason anything happens to us is because of our own state of mind. In other words, the equivalent is in our mind. If we are in a mood of loss and despair, we will attract loss along all lines. If we live in fear of being cheated, swindled, robbed, etc., we must realize that we attract what we fear. This is a cardinal and fundamental truth. Therefore, we must accept responsibility for what happens to us. Cease blaming others, for this habit will only compound the misery.

She Cured Her Jealousy

A young medical doctor said to me in Zurich, Switzerland, where I lectured recently, "I caught myself resenting and being jealous of one of my associates in the clinic. I read your book, *The Power of Your Subconscious Mind,** and asked myself: What am I doing to myself? My thoughts are creative. I am decreeing loss and limitation for myself. I am saying

*See *The Power of Your Subconscious Mind* by Dr. Joseph Murphy, Prentice-Hall, Inc., Englewood Cliffs, N.J., 1963.

that she can get promoted in the hospital and I can't. I am demoting myself. I stopped doing it."

She had done a little self-analysis, which is good for all of us. When you find yourself creating mental poisons, begin instead to feed on the bread of heaven, the bread of peace, harmony, love and goodwill to all. "I helped my brother's boat to the shore and, lo, my own boat was also at the shore."

She Stopped Stealing from Herself

A secretary had been brooding over the fact that she had been passed over for promotion. Another girl with far less experience had been promoted over her with a greater salary and greater prestige. She did not know that in this resentment she was actually stealing from herself.

The explanation is the cure. She began to understand that when she brooded over her loss and resented the gain or advancement of another and assigned the cause of her trouble entirely to others, she was stealing promotion, advancement and health from herself. Her mood of loss would attract even more loss and limitation.

I explained further to her that when she steals from herself in thought and feeling, this mental attitude will be confirmed and made manifest in some loss or demotion at the hands of others or events or negative situations.

She established peace in her mind and realized that

she promotes herself and no longer looks to others for promotion or advancement. She is now operating her own office in her home and is very successful. She adjusted her sense of values and triumphed in the art of living. Her experience was a great awakener to the powers of her own mind, which had been dormant.

The Trouble Was Within Himself

A high school boy had been sent by his parents for a consultation with me. I found that this young boy was full of deep-seated resentment toward his parents. It seems that his brother was a brilliant student who got excellent grades and commendations from his teachers. His parents were always praising his brother, but they never praised him or said kind things to him.

He was striking back in his own way. He joined a cult, which he knew would irritate them. He also began to smoke marijuana, which further infuriated his parents. He skipped school from time to time and went to a pool hall. He began to steal money from his mother, although he had a liberal allowance. Actually, he was trying to steal love.

Again, we come to the conclusion that the explanation is the cure. He began to become aware for the first time that his unconscious resentment and hostility toward his parents were burning up his own tissues and affecting him mentally and emotionally. He learned about the deleterious effects of marijuana on the cortical area of his brain, its degenerative effects on his sexual organs and the destructive effects on all organs of his body, as reported by the most outstanding medical experts here and abroad.

I talked with the parents of the boy and they changed their attitude. They ceased making invidious comparisons with his brother, which tends to excite envy and odium of the other, and he ceased being antisocial and stopped poisoning himself mentally and physically.

He is now practicing the mirror treatment, which consists of looking in the mirror in the morning and affirming for about five minutes: "I AM a son of the Living God. God loves me and cares for me. I exalt God in the midst of me." As he continues, this prayer will become a habit, and it is impossible to think of two things at the same time. When prone to get angry, all he has to do is to say: "I exalt God in the midst of me," and the angry or hateful thought is changed to constructive spiritual energy. He is on the way to great things.

Look Within Always for the Cause

I have talked with girls who have married men of a different race, religion and background for no other reason than to try to irritate and disgrace their parents. The trouble is that they do not know the Real Self—God—within.

When they learn to exalt the Divine Presence, the

Living Spirit, the Reality of them, they will auto-matically respect the Divinity in others. The criminal hates himself and projects that hatred on to others. He has never found his real Self, which is God, within him.

Boys and girls who were mistreated, neglected and unloved in their home life, become misfits, trouble makers at school, agitators and prone to fighting, stealing and lying. They are trying to get attention and recognition, but they get it the wrong way. They do not know that it is their state of mind that is playing havoc with them.

In truth, there is no one to change but ourselves. If we have the wrong attitude toward life and people, everything will go wrong. Realize that when you are Divinely guided, all of your ways will be ways of pleasantness and all of your paths will be peaceful and harmonious. Remember, you create your own success, happiness and peace of mind.

You are wise when you realize that your success and prosperity in life do not depend on what other people say or do, or do not say or do not do. Realize also that you were born to win, to succeed and triumph over all obstacles. Your success depends on your atti-tude of mind and your conviction about God, life and the universe. God is always successful in all of His undertakings, and God indwells you.

As you continue to know, feel and believe that you can do all things through the God-Power which strengtheneth you, you will find yourself going up the ladder of life irrespective of what others say or do, or do not say or do. Knowing that God is the Source of all your blessings, you will find yourself free of all jealousy, hate, resentment and hostility. Decide to look to the Infinite for all your good and you will never be disappointed.

You Can Call on Your Reserves

There is an inexhaustible reservoir of strength, wisdom and energy within your deeper mind. All armies on the march, for example, make sure that reserves are there when needed and can be called upon. This gives the general in charge a certain assurance and confidence.

God indwells you, and all the powers, attributes and qualities of God indwell each one of us. All of us live, move and have our being in that Infinite Being which created all things and is the very life of us. "There is," says Emerson, "guidance for each of us, and by lowly listening we shall hear the right words."

A girl who was attacked by a purse snatcher said, "God watches over me. He cares for me." Her attacker ran off. She called on her reserves and there was a response. This is a reciprocal universe; action and reaction are always and everywhere equal. In her emergency she called on the Almighty One and there was a response which set her free from the mugger.

Begin every day with your thought of God and His

love for you. Remember also a simple truth: The beginning of all manifestation or phenomena in this material universe is a thought or a word; and a word is a thought expressed. Your thought is first cause. God is the Creative Power in you, and the only immaterial power you know is your thought. Your thought is creative, and you are what you think all day long.

The Doctor Said She Was "Accident Prone"

A woman who frequently studied astrology magazines read that the signs indicated she might have an accident. She became full of fear and in rapid succession had three accidents with her automobile in one day. The next day she fell down and cut herself severely. She burned her hand cooking.

I explained to her that the dominant idea in her mind controlled all lesser thoughts, ideas, actions and reactions. Her dominant idea was that she would have an accident, and according to her belief it occurred.

She reversed her attitude of mind and decided to experience good fortune and Divine protection by affirming these great truths several times a day. The dominating thought of God's love watching over her and the whole armor of God enfolding her brings good fortune and determines her future.

Her belief determines her experience. . . . *Go thy way; and as thou hast believed, so be it done unto thee.* . . . (Matthew 8:13). Since it is done unto all of us according to our belief, it has nothing to do with the configuration of the stars or planets, or circumstances, conditions or events, or our genes, or any other thing on the face of the globe. Your belief is your state of mind. Accept the truth in your mind and gain strength and confidence.

This is the prayer the "accident prone" woman used, which reversed her state of mind and brought peace to her soul: "God is all there is. One with God is a majority. *If God be for me who can be against me?* (Romans 8:31). I know and believe that God is the Living Spirit Almighty—the Ever-Living One, the All-Wise One—and there is no power to challenge God. I know and accept completely that when my thoughts are God's thoughts, God's power is with my thoughts of good. I know I cannot receive what I cannot give, and I give out thoughts of love, peace, light and goodwill to this person or persons (mention name or names) and to everyone else. I am immunized and God-intoxicated, and I am always surrounded by the sacred circle of God's love. The whole armor of God surrounds me and enfolds me. I am Divinely guided and directed, and I enter into the joy of living. . . . *In thy presence is fulness of joy; at thy right hand there are pleasures for evermore* (Psalm 16:11)."

CHAPTER 10

The Book of Life

Phineas Parkhurst Quimby, America's greatest spiritual healer, said in 1847 that children are like little, white tablets upon which everybody who comes along scribbles something. All of us were born without any religious beliefs, fears, prejudices or racial bias. When we were children we were highly impressionable and malleable and subject to the teachings and beliefs of all those who had any control over our lives. Children grow up in the image and likeness of the dominant mental and emotional climate of the home. The first language you spoke came from your parents.

Your subconscious mind is a book of the law, and the dominant impressions and convictions of the mind become the ruling and governing forces of your life. In talking with and counselling many people through the years, I have found that the main reason many do not advance in life and remain healthy and prosperous is that when they were very young they had impressed on their deeper mind (the subconscious) feelings of inadequacy, unworthiness and inferiority, which governed their choices in life and their reactions, preventing them from succeeding and prospering in life.

Sigmund Freud, the great psychopathologist, pointed out that all of us are governed by subconscious impulses which are mostly irrational, which means that most of the religious beliefs, taboos and strictures which were given to us when very young are illogical, unreasonable, unscientific and completely contrary to basic common sense. One man, for example, said to me, "It's wrong for me to make so much money." Since he kept thinking that way, he eventually lost his business and did not know why. However, he learned the hard way that his subconscious takes what he says and thinks literally, and that whatever he conveyed to his subconscious mind would be made manifest, whether good or bad.

His family could have used the money and he could have done a lot of good with it, but this false and irrational impulse and belief in his subconscious governed his actions long after the earlier statements of his mother had been forgotten. He had to fail, because he was constantly reminding himself, "It is wrong to make so much money. Money is evil." This was a record implanted in his deeper mind, and it was being played back to him.

He learned that there is nothing good or bad, but thinking makes it so, and that there is nothing evil in the universe, for good and evil are the movements of his own mind relative to the One Being—God—the Living Spirit, which is whole, pure and perfect. Use determines whether a thing is good or evil. How do you use the Power? If you use the One Power constructively, you call It God, Allah, Brahma, peace, harmony and prosperity. If you use the One Power negatively, ignorantly or maliciously, you can experience lack, limitation, sickness and disease. The world calls it satan, devil, hell, etc., all of which are states of mind. The word *satan* means to err, to slip, to deviate from the truth.

As you continue to read this chapter, the truth will be revealed to you about the Book of Life. Remember, when a person is fearful, suspicious or angry, he acts and reacts in an abnormal way even when there are no circumstances or conditions warranting such actions. What is written in his Book of Life (his subconscious) becomes a law governing his experiences and relationships with others.

How Your Mind Works

The Book of Life is your subconscious mind, and you are always writing in that Book based on the nature of your habitual thinking and imagining. Shakespeare said, "What is in a name?" Well, when I mention your name, it indicates your particular sex, your nationality, your background, your training, your education, your financial structure, your social status, and all other things appertaining to you.

When your conscious and subconscious mind work harmoniously, peacefully and joyfully together, the children of that union are happiness, peace, health, abundance and security. The disharmonious relationship of the conscious and subconscious mind brings misery, suffering, pain, sickness and disease into your life.

Abram left Ur of Chaldea. Ur means sorcery, black magic, worship of stars, idols and all that sort of thing. Abram changed his name to Abraham, meaning the father of the multitude, indicating the one God, the one Presence and Power.

We are all children of the one God. That's the unity of all life. All men and women are brothers and sisters —same mind, same spirit and same substance. Therefore, to hurt another is to hurt yourself; and to bless another is to bless yourself.

You can write a new name, a new estimate and a new blueprint of yourself. Get a new concept of yourself. Is it great enough, noble enough or grand enough to redeem you, to bring about an inner transformation of your heart, your mind and your whole being? Today people have many idols just as they had in Chaldea thousands of years ago. Superstition is rampant. They still have false gods, such as "The weather is going to give me a cold," or "If I wet my feet I am going to get pneumonia." Some are afraid of germs, so that when someone sneezes, they feel they may be infected by the virus. If you ask the exposed person, "Did you get the virus this year?" the response is, "No, not yet." The infection is anticipated, though. What you expect, you always get.

Some people say, "I don't know the right congressman. I have no pull. I can't get that job." They are thus denying the Creative Power within them. They say It is omnipotent and supreme, yet at the same time they are denying It. If It is supreme and omnipotent, there is nothing to oppose It or challenge It. Therefore, you should say, "Infinite Spirit opens up the door for me, revealing to me my hidden talents and showing me the way I should go." That's exactly what the Infinite Spirit will do for you.

There are congressmen who speak and touch wood when they talk about something negative, as if the wood had some power. Do you give power to other people? To the atmosphere? To the weather? All of these things are innocuous. They have no power. The power is in you.

Changing Your Name

Saul's name was changed to Paul. The meaning of Paul is the "Little Christ," and many miracles were wrought by the hand of Paul. Paul was illumined on the road to Damascus, which means a sack of blood, or rebirth. This means a mystical illumination where your mind, or intellect, is flooded with the light of God and you are a transformed man. Sometimes this takes place in the twinkling of an eye, like that which St. Theresa and many others experienced.

Paul became a changed man. He was no longer the murderer who sent people to death. He was transformed. He was illumined from On High. You can go to court and change your name every year if you wish. However, it doesn't mean anything. It is absolutely meaningless, as a matter of fact. You must change your nature, your disposition, your viewpoint and your concept of yourself. There must be an inner transformation. Then, of course, you will have really changed your name, or your nature.

Some time ago a man came to see me who was a "sourpuss," and who was cynical and who would habitually snarl at his secretary and at the salesman when he came in. If someone said, "It's a good day," he would say, "What's good about it?" And when he came down to breakfast in the morning, he would hold the paper up in front of himself lest he might see his wife. He would always criticize the bacon and the eggs. He was just a plain sourpuss—nasty and ugly.

He practiced the following instruction: "When you come down in the morning, kiss your wife and tell her she looks lovely and the food is delicious, and she'll probably faint." The man said, "Well, I'll be a hypocrite if I do that." I said, "Go ahead. Start it, anyhow. Break the ice in your heart, and when you go into the office, tell the secretary how beautiful her hair is, or her eyes. There must be something lovely about her. And be genial, courteous and affable to the salesman."

After a month's time, as he practiced these things, they gradually sank into his subconscious mind and he became transformed—genial, affable, amiable and philosophical. People said, "What happened to that fellow?" Others said, "He's in love." Well, I guess he was—in love with the Higher Self.

"He that guided me this far will open up the rest of the way." That's a magnificent truth. A teacher wrote me from Alabama, and I gave him that simple truth. He said that his building was three-quarters finished and now there was a strike; he did not have the money, and what was he going to do? "He that guided me this far will open up the rest of the way."

He said, "That is not correct. You should say, 'He *who* guided me will open up the rest of the way.'" I said, "No. I meant that literally." It was not a slip. It was deliberate, because I am dealing with a principle, an impersonal Presence which is no respecter of persons, a universal Presence and Power available to all men. The cutthroat, beggar, thief, holy man, atheist, or agnostic—any man can tap It. Any man can use It.

God is not a person, so we don't say, "Our Father, who art in Heaven." We say, "Our Father, *which* art in Heaven," indicating an impersonal Presence and Power—an Infinite Life and an Infinite Intelligence. So, you see, he had a concept of a God-man up in the sky somewhere. He practiced, however, what I taught him to do, and he found that he attracted the necessary funds to complete the building.

What Do You Believe?

This Universal Presence creates out of Itself by means of It becoming that particular thing. In other words, God becomes man by believing Himself to be man. God creates a being out of Himself capable of returning glory, light and love to Himself. Abraham knew the Creative Power. He was aware of It, and he demonstrated It in his life. He believed that the Spirit would guide and direct him, which, of course, It did.

Plato, Aristotle, Plotinus, etc., all spoke of God as Infinite Mind and Infinite Intelligence, but they did not tell you how to use the Presence and Power for guidance, for harmony, for prosperity, for success, or how to heal yourself with it. It was a satisfactory intellectual conclusion—very interesting, but they did not tell you how to use It in everyday practice.

If you believe you are an abject worm of the dust, people will step on you and will treat you the way you treat yourself. If you are cruel and nasty to yourself, the world will be cruel and nasty to you. As within, so without. Realize that you are a son or a daughter of the Living God. You are heir to all of God's riches. Realize you should exalt God in the midst of you, mighty to heal. How could you feel inferior if you knew that you were a daughter of the Infinite, that you were a darling of God, and that God loves you and cares for you? God is the Life Principle, or the Living Spirit within you, which created you and watches over you when you are sound asleep, because He that watches over you neither slumbers nor sleeps.

Born to Win

There are a great many people who work very hard, but they nevertheless fail in life. The reason is that they have a subconscious pattern of failure, or they believe they should fail. Sometimes they think a jinx is following them. They feel inferior. Perhaps they were told when they were young, "You'll never amount to anything. You are stupid. You are dumb." These thoughts were accepted by their impressionable mind and now these thoughts have a life of their own in the subconscious mind, and are experienced by them.

But man can change his life. These subconscious or irrational impulses act long after the events which caused them have been forgotten. Man can feed the subconscious mind with something new. He can say, "I'm born to succeed; the Infinite cannot fail." He can feed his subconscious life-giving patterns such as: "Divine law and order govern my life, Divine peace fills my soul, Divine love saturates my mind, Divine right action reigns supreme, Infinite Intelligence guides and directs me in all my ways—It is a lamp unto my feet and a light upon my path."

When you are angry, suspicious or full of fear, these emotions are negative and destructive. They snarl

174

up in the subconscious mind, and they cause you to do the wrong thing and to say the wrong thing. When you want to be happy, you are sad; when you want to do the right thing, you do the wrong thing. This is true when you are under the sway of negative and destructive emotions, for, very likely, whatever you do then will be wrong.

The Seven Seals

So, you can write a new name in the book of life. The book of life, as previously explained to you, is the law of your own subconscious. The Bible says, *I saw in the right hand of him that sat on the throne a book written within and on the backside, sealed with seven seals. And I saw a strong angel proclaiming with a loud voice, Who is worthy to open the book, and to loose the seals thereof? And no man in heaven, nor in earth, neither under the earth, was able to open the book, neither to look thereon. And I wept much, because no man was found worthy to open and to read the book, neither to look thereon* (Revelation 5:1-4).

Now, the book written within and on the backside is your objective and subjective mind. You have a conscious and subconscious mind. Whatever thoughts, beliefs, theories, opinions or dogmas you write, engrave or impress on your subconscious mind, you experience as objective manifestations, as circumstances, conditions and events. What we write on the inside we experience on the outside. We have two sides of our lives—objective and subjective, visible and invisible, thought and its manifestation.

The seven seals are the seven states of consciousness. Our concept passes through seven degrees of awareness whereby we spiritualize our five senses by turning inward to the spiritual Power. Then we get our conscious and subconscious mind to agree and synchronize. When there is no longer any doubt in your conscious or subconscious mind, your prayer is always answered. You break the seven seals when you discipline your five senses and get the two phases of your mind to agree.

There are seven seals. The first is sight. This means to see the truth about any situation. See perfect health where sickness is; see harmony where discord is; love where hatred is. Then you are seeing the truth and you are disciplining your faculty of sight.

The second is hearing. You hear the glad tidings, the truth of God. You hear your mother tell you what you long to hear—that the miracle of God has happened—that she is healed. In other words, you do not see her in a hospital as being ill. You hear the opposite. You hear her tell you about her perfect health. Then you are hearing the truth.

The third is smell. You smell the truth by coming to a definite decision, realizing that God who made your body can also heal it. You reject all other food unfit for mental consumption. A dog smells food; if it is unsavory, he rejects it. Likewise, reject all thoughts, ideas and opinions that do not fill your soul with joy.

The fourth is taste. You taste the sweet savor of God. You taste the truth by appropriating the ideas or truths of God in your mind through meditation, reading and through frequent occupancy of the mind regarding the perfect outcome you want.

The fifth is the joy you feel when you touch mentally and emotionally the answered prayer, while feeling the reality of it.

The remaining two seals are your conscious and subconscious mind. When you succeed in disciplining the five senses, the male and female principle in your own mind begins to interact harmoniously. A Divine marriage takes place between your desire and your emotion, and a child comes forth from the union, which is the joy of the answered prayer.

That is the book of life that people are talking about. If someone could photograph your subconscious mind, they would see your future, your past and your present thinking. The future is your present thoughts grown up. However, you can always change the future by changing the present. Feast on whatsoever things are true, lovely, noble and God-like. Think these thoughts with conviction. The old thoughts will die. They will fade away. They will be obliterated, expunged from your deeper mind, because the lower is subject to the higher.

Think of everything lovely and of good report. Get new thoughts and ideas regarding principles and the eternal verities. Remember, your subconscious mind does not accept your idle wishes, dreams or hopes.

Instead, it accepts your convictions—what you really, sincerely believe deep down in your heart.

What do you believe? Do you believe in the goodness of God in the land of the living, and the guidance of God, and the harmony of God, and the love of God, and the abundance of God? If you do, all of these things will come to pass, because to believe is to live in the state of being it. It is to accept something as true.

Who Are You?

Look at your spiritual heritage. We are all children of the I AM, as Moses says. Within you is the real nature or the real name, because you are pronouncing it all day long. I AM. It is called Om in India. The Bible says, *I AM THAT I AM* (Exodus 3:14). Moses said, *I AM hath sent me unto you* (Exodus 3:14).

Realize that I AM sent you to your business tomorrow, to a tough assignment, to solve it, to overcome it. The engineer, when he meets with a pressing problem, realizes I AM has sent him there to solve the problem. The engineer grapples with the problem courageously and sees the solution.

We are all children of the I AM (God). Whatever you attach to I AM, you become. If you say, "I am no good, I'm a flop, I'm a failure, I'm going deaf, I'm going blind, I'm nobody," then you become what you affirm. Therefore, reverse it and say, "I am happy, joyous and free. I am illumined; I am inspired. I am strong; I am powerful. 'Let the weak say, I am strong.' 'Let the widow say, it is well.' I am a son or daughter of the Living God. I am heir to all of God's riches. I am born to win and to succeed, for the Infinite cannot fail. I am a tremendous success. I am absolutely outstanding. I am unique, and there is no one in all the world like me."

Why don't you claim the above and write these truths in your heart and inscribe them in your inward parts? *He that hath an ear, let him hear what the Spirit saith unto the churches* (Revelation 2:29). . . . *To him that overcometh will I give to eat of the hidden manna, and will give him a white stone, and in the stone a new name written, which no man knoweth saving he that receiveth it* (Revelation 2:17).

Manna is a symbol for the bread of Heaven. *I am the living bread which came down from Heaven . . .* (John 6:51). It is the bread of peace, of harmony; it is the blessed bread of God. Eat this bread of inspiration and guidance, for no man can live in the world today without spiritual food. You may sit down to dinner and have the choicest food but still be hungry for peace, harmony, love, inspiration and guidance.

Manna is a symbol of inspiration, of strength, of power and of wisdom. It will feed you in the desert of loneliness, of unhappiness, because the greatest desert of the world is not the Sahara; it is under the hat of man. Often there is very little growing there but weeds of ignorance, fear and superstition. Buddha asked

179

God the cause of all misery, suffering, crime and sickness in the world. The answer he received was "ignorance," for ignorance is the only sin and all punishment is the consequence.

Call on this Presence and Power. It will answer you. It will be with you in trouble. It will set you On High, because you hath known Its name or nature. The nature of Infinite Intelligence is to respond to you. Turn within to the Fountain of Life and feel refreshed from the standpoint of truth. You can be replenished there. . . . *Come ye to the waters, and he that hath no money; come ye, buy, and eat; yea, come, buy wine and milk without money and without price* (Isaiah 55:1). The price is to honor God and to believe in Him. That is the only price you pay.

If you do not honor God and recognize Him, it is just the same as if the Presence were not there. You can eat of the bread of peace, of joy, of faith and of confidence in the only Power there is. Your confidence and faith should not be in creeds, dogmas and traditions. Believe that whatever you impress on your subconscious will be expressed as form, function, experience and event. Then you will be learning to know yourself a little better.

A new name is a new disposition, a new perspective, a new insight. You can affirm, "God loves me and cares for me. I am illumined from On High." You can claim right action. You can claim, "The wisdom of God anoints my intellect and I am now writing this with my conscious pen into my subconscious mind. Whatever I inscribe in my subconscious mind becomes effective and functional."

Discover Yourself

You are here to solve problems. The reason you have problems and challenges is because you are here to discover your Divinity and sharpen your mental and spiritual tools; otherwise you would never discover yourself.

There are failures in life, yes! That is why you had an eraser at the end of your pencil when you went to school. Everybody knew that you were going to make mistakes. Through the mistakes, however, you learned how to add and subtract, as well as many, many other things.

You must have a basis for thinking constructively. When you know that thoughts are things and that what you feel you attract, and that what you imagine you become, then you begin to think constructively because you realize, "My thought is creative—not because it is my thought, but because it is thought."

"Nothing can give you peace but the triumph of principles" (Emerson). Quimby said that a child is like a little, blank tablet; and the uncles, and the aunts, and the clergyman and everybody else comes along and scribbles something on it. This is easy to do because the little child's mind, of course, is impressionable, malleable and open to all of the beliefs, opinions, creeds, dogmas, superstition, ignorance and fear of the parents. The child grows up in the image and the likeness of the dominant mental, emotional and spiritual climate of the home.

Who is scribbling on your mind today? Does your mother-in-law, father-in-law or some in-law scribble something on your mind? Do they disturb you? Does someone tell you you are going to fail? And do you reject it and say, "You do not know what you are talking about. I cannot fail. How could I fail? The Infinite is within me. I am born to win. I am a success in my prayer life, in my relationship with people, and in my chosen work." The minute you affirm the above, the Power will respond to you.

How could the Infinite fail? Where is the Infinite? Within you. And you are born to win, to overcome, to triumph. You are here to go from glory to glory, and from octave to octave, for there is no end to the glory which is man.

Is the columnist writing something in your mind? Or are you writing the truths of God, which are the same yesterday, today and forever? What are you writing in your mind every day? Some people write grief, despair, hopelessness, loneliness, etc. Inscribe the conviction that you are worthy, that you are adequate, that you are full of faith and confidence in the only Power there is, and that you know you are inspired from On High, and that you believe implicitly that God is guiding you in all your ways and is a lamp unto your feet and a light upon your path.

Your subconscious mind, which is the book of life, will receive these impressions, viewpoints, opinions and convictions because you are sincere, because you mean them. Whatever you think, feel and believe to be true, your subconscious mind will bring to pass— good or bad.

Inscribe in your mind harmony, health, wholeness, beauty, peace, perfection and right action. These are principles. You do not create these truths, but you activate them and make them effective and functional when you affirm them. Stir up the gifts of God within you.

Anything that fills you with faith, with confidence, with joy and with enthusiasm has power over you, and it governs your conduct. Enthusiasm governs all of your activities, because enthusiasm means "possessed by God." You will never go so far as when you are possessed by the One, the Beautiful and the Good.

You are a mental and a spiritual being, because when you say I AM, you are announcing the Presence of the Living God. You have always lived. A billion years from now you will be alive, because life was never born and will never die; water wets it not, fire burns it not, wind blows it not away. You are alive, and that life is God's life. God is life; therefore, you have always lived.

Are you the same person you were five years ago? Ten years ago? Twenty-five years ago? No, you are not. Are you the same person you were when you were three months old or a year old? Of course not. You have had hundreds of reincarnations since you were born. Reincarnation is Spirit making Itself manifest at higher levels. So, at five years of age you were different; at 10, at 20, and at 30. If I showed you photographs of every month of your life, you would hardly recognize yourself in some of them.

You are not the same as you were six months ago. You have a new concept of God, of Life, of the universe—a new estimate, a new blueprint, a new insight. You do not talk the same; you do not walk the same or think the same. Your life is progressing from glory to glory. When you go on to the next dimension, you will still go on from octave to octave. You cannot be less tomorrow than you are today, for life goes not backward nor tarries with yesterday.

Write, "I go from glory to glory. I go from octave to octave." Write these truths in your life, because you are alive and you are always implanting something new in your deeper mind.

Lake of Fire

I receive many letters, a few of which say, "You will be cast into a lake of fire because you are telling people on your radio program that each man is his own saviour, that God indwells him, and that all he has to do is contact this God-Presence and It will lead him, guide him and solve his problems for him. You also say that every man answers his own prayers. Some day you will burn in the lake of fire for all eternity for saying these things." Then they quote the

184

Bible by saying, *"For God so loved the world, that He gave his only begotten Son, that whosoever believeth in him should not perish, but have everlasting life"* (John 3:16).

All of this is based on a lack of understanding, however. Everybody is the only begotten Son. We are all begotten of the Only One. There is Only One. Your only begotten Son, spiritually speaking, is your desire. If you are sick, health is your saviour. You have a desire for health. Realization of your desire is your saviour. If you are lost in the woods, guidance is your saviour. If you are imprisoned, freedom is your saviour. If you are dying of thirst, water is your saviour. So, every man who is able to contact the God-Presence is, of course, his own saviour.

The late of fire mentioned in the Bible is no literal fire, of course. The Bible is a spiritual book. It is speaking in spiritual, mental, allegorical, figurative, idiomatic and mystical language. If you should go to a hospital to the psychotic ward, or to any other mental institution, you will find people there burning in the lake of fire. The lake, of course, is your subconscious mind. The fire means they are seething with jealousy, hate, resentment, hostility and anger. They are burning up their tissues and their hearts with these negative emotions.

A psychotic is tormented, isn't he? He is on fire with his own misery. Some people are on fire with their own hatred, resentment, hostility, etc. Of course, they are living in a lake of fire created by themselves, because every man creates his own hell and his own heaven. Omar said:

> I sent my soul to the Invisible
> Some letter of the After-Life to spell;
> And by and by my soul returned to me,
> Saying, "I, myself, am heaven and hell."

Anger, depression, fear and foreboding are the inner fires. Any doctor will tell you that these emotions give you ulcers, high blood pressure, cancer and arthritis. Hate can give you arthritis if you keep it up; it will bring about physical changes, bring on calcareous deposits in your tissues and play general havoc with you. Sometimes jealousy will drive a person absolutely insane, because there is no more destructive poison than jealousy. It is called the green-eyed monster and is the greatest of all mental poisons.

Therefore, sow for yourself treasures in heaven, where the moth and the rust doth not consume, and where thieves cannot break through and steal. Sow for yourself harmony, health, peace and beauty. Write in your heart the truths of God. What will you write? Write . . . *whatsoever things are true, whatsoever things are honest, whatsoever things are just, whatsoever things are pure, whatsoever things are lovely, whatsoever things are of good report; if there be any virtue, and if there be any praise, think on these things* (Philippians 4:8).

186

CHAPTER 11

Why Are You Here?

Every man's life from beginning to end is a plan of God. Jesus said, "I am come that they might have life . . . more abundantly." You are here to lead a full, happy and glorious life. You are here to release your hidden talents to the world, to find your true place in life and to express yourself at your highest level.

Finding Your True Place

A young woman came to see me some months ago and said, "I'm a misfit. No one wants me. I'm a square peg in a round hole." I explained to her that each person is unique and that no two people are alike, any more than are two crystals of snow or two leaves of a tree. God never repeats Himself; infinite differentiation is the law of life. There is no such thing as an unneeded person. I quoted Emerson for her, wherein he said, "I am an organ of God and God hath need of me where I am; otherwise I would not be here."

She asked, "What is it God wishes me to do?"

The answer is simple. And the prayer that she used

to follow God's Will also is simple, direct and to the point.

Her Special Prayer

"God reveals to me my hidden talents and whispers into my heart the thing He wants me to do. I know that God is Infinite Intelligence and is seeking expression through me. I am a focal point of Infinite Life in the same way that an electric bulb is a focal point for the manifestation of electricity. God flows through me as harmony, health, peace, joy, growth and expansion along all lines. I recognize the *lead* which comes into my conscious, reasoning mind, and I give thanks for the answer now."

After a few days a deep urge came to her to take a certain business course, which she is now ardently pursuing, and undoubtedly she will be a great success.

Claim Your Good Now

Now is the accepted time. Many people are always looking forward to the future for better times. They are constantly saying that some day they will be happy and successful, instead of realizing that God is the Eternal Now!

The truth is that all the powers of the Godhead are within you. Peace is now; you can claim that God's river of peace flows through you. Healing is now; feel and know that the infinite healing Presence which made you is now restoring every atom of your being. Claim that the creative Intelligence which made you knows how to heal you, and that Divine order governs your mind and body.

Wealth is available now—it is a thought-image in your mind. Claim it boldly now. Affirm: "God's wealth is now circulating in my life." Why wait for it?

Strength is now. Call on the power of God within you, and this power will respond, energizing and renewing your whole being.

Love is now. Know and believe that God's love saturates your mind and body, and this Divine love will be filtered through and made manifest in all phases of your life.

Guidance is now. Infinite Intelligence within you knows the answer, and it responds to the nature of your request.

Claim your good *now*. You do not create anything; you give form and expression to that which always was, now is and ever shall be. Moses could have used a loud speaker or television. The idea or principle by which these are made always existed in Infinite Mind. Plato referred to the "archetypes of Divine Mind," which simply means that there is an idea or a pattern in Divine Mind behind every created thing in the universe.

The Present Moment

Did you ever stop to think that if you are planning something in the future, you are planning it now? If you are fearing something in the future, you are fearing it now. If you are thinking of the past, you are

189

thinking of it now. The only thing you have to change is your present thought. You are aware of your present thought, and all that you can realize is the outer manifestation of your habitual thinking at the present moment. The two thieves are the past and the future. If you are indulging in remorse or self-criticism over past mistakes and hurts, the mental anguish you experience is the pain of your present thought. If you are worried about the future, you are robbing and stealing from yourself joy, health and happiness. Count your blessings now and get rid of the two thieves.

To think of a happy and joyful episode in the past is a present joy. Remember, the results of past events —good or bad—are but the representatives of your present thinking. Direct your present thought in the right channels. Enthrone in your mind peace, harmony, joy, love, prosperity and goodwill. Dwell consciously on these concepts and claim them—and forget all other things. *Finally, brethren, whatsoever things are true . . . honest . . . just . . . pure . . . lovely . . . of good report; if there be any virtue, and if there be any praise, think on these things* (Philippians 4:8).

He Stopped Blaming Providence

Recently a man told me of his many troubles and ended up by blaming God for all his reverses. I explained to him that the universe is one of law and order, and that God is, among other things, Principle or Law, and that if man breaks a law, he will suffer accordingly. It is not punishment by an angry God. On the contrary, it is an *impersonal* matter of cause and effect. If he misuses the Law of Mind, the reaction will be negative; but if he uses the law correctly, it will help him and heal him and restore his soul.

I suggested ideas on how to become a free-flowing channel for Divine Life and gave him the following prayer to use frequently:

"I am a clear, open channel of the Divine, and Infinite Life flows unobstructedly through me as health, peace, prosperity and right action. I am constantly releasing new, creative ideas, setting free the imprisoned splendor within."

This man has had a new lease on life and has told me that he now is beginning to live. He added ruefully, "I stopped blocking my good. I have taken my foot off the hose and the waters of Life are flowing abundantly into my life." He has learned to relax, and he has ceased pressing the weight of his negative mentality upon the infinite "pipeline" of life.

One Life Principle

There is only one Life Principle animating the entire universe. God is Life and that is your life now, but this Life Principle may be directed constructively or destructively, because you have the ability to choose.

You are using the Life Principle destructively whenever you indulge in fear, regret or any form of negative thinking. All resentment, hostility, spiritual pride, self-will, criticism and condemnation are especially disastrous methods of misapplying the Life Principle. Furthermore, the negative emotions which are dammed up in our subconscious come forth as all manner of diseases, both mental and physical.

When you tune in with the Infinite and let it flow through you harmoniously and joyously, and when you think right, feel right and act right, your life will be one of unalloyed happiness and success along all lines —right here and now.

Why She Failed to Prosper

A young school teacher complained to me that she was getting no results even though she prayed regularly for prosperity and success. I discovered while talking with her that unconsciously she was always rehearsing her troubles, criticizing and blaming the pupils, the parents and the school authorities. I pointed out to her that she was actually squandering the treasures of life within her on negative thoughts that were destructive. She reversed her attitude of mind and affirmed frequently with deep understanding:

" 'God hath not given me the spirit of fear; but of power, and of love, and of a sound mind.' I have a firm, unwavering faith in God as my bountiful, ever-present Good. I am vitalized and prospered in all my ways. Promotion is mine now. Peace is mine now. I radiate love and goodwill to all my pupils, my associates and to all those around me. From the depths of my heart I wish for all of them peace, joy and happiness. The intelligence and wisdom of God animate and sustain all those in my classes at all times, and I am illumined and inspired. When I am tempted to think negatively, I will immediately think of God's healing love."

Within a month this teacher had established harmony in all her relationships and received her promotion.

Divine Discontent

You are here to reproduce all the qualities and aspects of God. Inasmuch as this is the true reason for your existence, it behooves you to have a wholesome dissatisfaction with anything less than complete harmony, health and peace of mind. An inquietude regarding frustration, lack and limitation should become a great incentive to you, enabling you to overcome all difficulties through the Infinite Power within you. Your joy is in overcoming. Problems, difficulties and challenges of life enable you to sharpen your mental and spiritual tools, enabling you to release the treasures of the infinite storehouse of riches within.

Infinite Mind is spaceless and timeless. Cease limiting yourself. Remove all stumbling blocks which are in your mind and enter *now* into the joy of the answered prayer. . . . *Lift up your eyes, and look on the fields; for they are white already to harvest* (John 4:35).

CHAPTER 12

The Meaning of Satan, Devil, Serpent, Etc.

There is only One Power. *Hear, O Israel: The Lord our God is one Lord* (Deuteronomy 6:4). Then, since God alone *is,* the devil *is not.* Since God is Being, the devil is not-Being. In other words, the devil does not exist. As Judge Troward points out so lucidly in his *Bible Mystery and Bible Meaning:* "It is precisely this fact of non-existence that makes up the devil; it is that power which in appearance is, and in reality is not; in a word, it is the power of the negative."

The Eye Was Called the Devil

In the ancient Tarot teaching, the Hebrew mystics referred to the devil as Ayin, which is the 16th letter in the Hebrew alphabet and spelled oin in Hebrew. It means the eye as an instrument of sight. It also stands for mirth. The eye is concerned only with the surface appearance of things. People used to say, "The sun rises in the east and sets in the west" and "The earth is flat and does not move." Yet, science has now convinced people how faulty the eye is in this respect:

THE MEANING OF SATAN

The sun does not rise and set, the earth is not flat and the earth does not stand still. For example, science today makes it clear that we do not see anything as it really is. This is a universe of densities, frequencies and intensities. Your body is plastic, porous and pliable. It is simply composed of waves of light and of atoms and molecules swirling around at tremendous speed. Our eyes are geared to see three-dimensionally.

The Hebrew secret wisdom knew more than modern science about the illusory nature of matter, as well as the limitations of our eyes. Hence, the attribution of mirth to the letter Ayin, which means the eye. Remember, Ayin refers to what seems rather than to what is, with illusion rather than reality. This is why mirth is associated with the word *devil*. The real meaning of the word *devil* in Hebrew mysticism is *the slanderer* —one who tells lies about God. The eye slanders the fact because it deals only with the outside appearance of a fact.

God Upside-Down

The ancient Hebrew mystics who wrote the Bible said that the devil is God upside-down. In other words, the devil is God as He is misunderstood by ignorant and primitive people. The devil of theologians does not exist; it was created by them to account for the evil in the world. Evil, however, comes from our misunderstanding or misuse and misapplication of the One Power.

We are choosing, volitional beings and we are here to evolve and learn the laws of life and to apply them correctly. Anything misapprehended or misapplied constitutes evil. If you do not choose the good, then you will experience the negative reaction from your subconscious mind because of your wrong choice.

Man's Invention

Theologians have accounted to the populace for the presence of evil by the invention of a devil. As for the gospels (the earliest is about 300 A.D.), the word *devil* is not found in the earlier versions. It occurs there as *a spirit of evil*. In the teaching of Jesus there is no mention of the theological devil, which was later invented by the church. Further, the word translated as *devil* is *a spirit of evil*, not *the spirit of evil*.

He went around expelling the devils, which are negative thought-forms of hate, jealousy, hostility, resentment, vengeance, self-condemnation and self-pity. These are the devils which harass us and are created by ourselves based on the way we think and feel. These negative emotions are, certainly, spirits (feelings) of evil.

"The essense of hell," says Swedenborg, "is the desire to control another." The devils are negative, destructive thought-forms, which result in negative, destructive emotions compelling the person to act them out. Negative, destructive emotions hidden in the subconscious must have an outlet resulting in all manner of chaos and suffering.

THE MEANING OF SATAN

Pain Is a Consequence

All the pain and suffering in the world are the consequence of our own thinking and misuse of the One Power, brought on by ourselves. There is no punishment dealt out by an angry God. God has nothing whatever to do with our suffering or sickness. To say that God is angry with us instead of regarding us with love and compassion is the greatest of blasphemies.

Conquering Obstacles

All of us are here to overcome obstacles, challenges, difficulties and problems, which enables us to discover the Divinity within us so that we can achieve our ends. The Greek word for *devil* is *diabolos, one who throws across* (problems and obstacles); and we are supposed to use them as stepping stones to our triumph and success. This is the way we progress and advance up the ladder of life.

The Fall of Lucifer

How art thou fallen from heaven, O Lucifer, son of the morning! how art thou cut down to the ground, which didst weaken the nations! (Isaiah 14:12). Lucifer means *Light,* or *I AM,* Which is God. God limits Himself when He becomes man. Lucifer falling from heaven is simply Spirit, God or I AM becoming matter; and our limitation is the so-called devil. The fall of Lucifer, which is the fall of God or Spirit becoming matter, really enables us to grow and release the spiritual powers within us. These challenges and difficulties in life sharpen our mental and spiritual tools, enabling us to discover our God-like powers so that we can rise, transcend and grow, thereby releasing more and more of God's qualities within us.

One Creative Power

Over and over again, the Bible stresses that there is but One Power, not two, not three, not a hundred, but One. Read these words from the Bible: *See now that I, even I, am he, and there is no god with me; I kill, and I make alive; I wound, and I heal . . .* (Deuteronomy 32:39).

This means that you can use the power two ways. This, of course, applies to any power in the world. You can use electricity to vacuum the floor or light up the house, but you can also use it to electrocute someone. In similar manner, you can use water to drown a child or quench his thirst. We have had floods here in California which have destroyed houses and ruined roads and bridges; however, when these waters are dammed and controlled, the water can be used to irrigate the land, light the cities and bless humanity in countless ways.

Scientists are now working on a process of splitting off the hydrogen from water, and the release of this energy will work miracles in our industrial life. The forces of nature are not evil. It depends on how we use them. The way we use any power is based upon our thought. Good and bad are, therefore, determined by the thoughts of man, his motivation and how he plans to use the powers of his mind and the forces of nature.

Good and evil are the movements of man's own mind relative to the One Supreme Power, Which is perfect in Itself. Think good and good follows; think evil and evil follows.

Lucifer, mentioned in the fourteenth chapter of Isaiah, refers also to man's false concept of God or I AM within him. Many people are willing to die for their superstitions and false beliefs rather than to open their minds and hearts to the Truths of Life. They are hard, unyielding and inflexible, and it seems to be impossible for them to give up the old, encrusted false beliefs about God and the law of life.

The Bible, in the fourteenth chapter of Isaiah, refers to their intransigent and intractable attitude of mind: *For thou hast said in thine heart, I will ascend into heaven, I will exalt my throne above the stars of God* . . . (Isaiah 14:13).

Some months ago a woman wrote me fourteen pages, pointing out that there is, indeed, a devil, a satan, who tempts people, brings on wars, possesses people's minds and causes crime, etc. It was no use reasoning with her superstition, false beliefs and dogmatic statements. Many people act that way. They exalt the so-called devil, or false beliefs, in their mind and dethrone God. The communist nations have exalted their theories above the stars (truths) of God also and are rebellious in their attitude, claiming that there is no God, but Lenin.

Truth Sets You Free

The minute you cast out from your mind the idea of any other power but the One, your false concept of God will fall from the throne of your mind; and you will realize that when you use the Power constructively, It is called God, which brings health and happiness into your life. When you use the Power negatively and ignorantly, it is called the devil, which brings misery, lack and suffering into your experience. Ignorance is also called the devil, which is a negation of life.

Archangel Lucifer

Lucifer, Satan, devil and serpent all mean the same thing. You have heard the story that the archangel Lucifer was cast into hell for his revolt against God. This, of course, is a pure myth. The Bible refers to Lucifer as the bright and morning star. . . . *I am the root and offspring of David, and the bright and morning star* (Revelation 22:16). The greatest star in all the world is the I AM within you, Which is God, or the Light of the whole world.

Hebrew Symbolism Referring to the So-Called Devil

The Hebrew seers who wrote the Bible were past masters in the art of psychology and the story of the soul, and they revealed the hidden meanings of the Bible in the Cabala. The Cabala is a mystical interpretation of the Bible and is the key to the allegories, numbers and symbolisms in the Bible.

In the ancient Tarot teaching, they devised a symbolic card setting forth that the devil came out of the distorted, twisted imagination of man. This imaginary being has goat's horns, a human head, donkey's ears and the wings of a bat. The upper part of the gross body is human, the thighs animal, the legs human and ending in eagle's claws.

Bat wings symbolize darkness, or ignorance. The horns are those of a goat because they show the backbone curves and cannot stand erect. (Man should walk uprightly in the Law.) The head has donkey's ears because man will not listen to the voice of intuition and refuses to hear and listen to the eternal verities. In other words, he is as obtuse and stubborn as a donkey.

The human part of the body is gross, indicating an absence of grace and beauty. The raised hand in the card blessing the pair (man and woman) is open wide as if to say that all there is to life is the desire for sensation; there is nothing else. The thighs are not human, but animal, indicating that man is following his instincts instead of the spiritual impulses. The legs indicate the negative emotions and passions which are governing him.

The legs end in eagle's claws. This refers to sexual abuse and misapplication of the sex urge. The upraised paw is a symbol of Saturn, indicating they are governed by their limitation.

Over the head of this devil is a pentagram, which is inverted. The five-pointed stars symbolize the perfected man. It should stand on two points, the conscious and subconscious as equals. Here it stands on one point. In other words, man is governed by his subconscious false beliefs, opinions and negative emotions. The symbol of the torch means that he is inflaming his passions and appetites.

Furthermore, he has malformed the woman, meaning that the conscious mind has polluted the subconscious. The left shoulder of the woman is lacking. Shoulders indicate emotion. The man and the woman (the male and female principles in all of us) are bound by chains to the half cube, on which the so-called devil squats. A cube represents the physical world. A half a cube represents half-knowledge, or ignorance. This is why the cube is black.

The man and the woman in the card have horns, hoofs and tails to signify that they are living entirely under negative emotions. The tail of the man is shaped like a scorpion, denoting that his principal bestiality is sex perversion. Her tail is a bunch of grapes, indicating that it is the business of the subconscious to bring to fruit the desires of the subconscious mind. The green grapes indicate negative use of imagination.

The devil has a navel, as have the man and the

woman. This is one of the most subtle symbolisms of the Tarot. The Tarot, regardless of how much these cards have been prostituted and abused, reveals how the laws of God work out in the cosmos and in man. The navel, of course, indicates that the devil is man-made.

Some of these marvelous symbols of the Tarot were presented to me by an outstanding student of the Tarot, Ann Mussmann, in New York City in 1943. I realized that they coincided with the Bible in every respect.

Thought Is Creative

Every thought tends to manifest itself. If your thought is of a negative nature, the Bible calls this the devil or Satan, the same old serpent which beguiled Eve in the garden. You must remember that it is impossible for there to be an infinite and universal power of evil, for unless the Infinite and Universal Power were creative, nothing could exist. God is the Life-Principle in all of us and is always seeking to express Itself. To suppose the Life-Principle acting other than life-giving would contradict the very nature of Its Being, Which is livingness and givingness.

There Is No Death

Life, or God, cannot die, and that life is your life now. Man believes in what he calls death; therefore, he experiences what he calls death. But, as Dr. Quimby said, in 1847, death is in us; the other person has simply passed on to the next dimension and is as much alive as we are. To say that death is the will of God is most emphatically denied by the Bible, for it says that . . . *him that had the power of death, that is, the devil* (Hebrews 2:14), or the false belief of the mass mind.

You might say that man dies and his body disintegrates. Disintegration is the breaking up of what was previously an integer or perfect whole, the separation of its component parts. Man then puts on a new fourth-dimensional body, which is rarefied and attenuated and which functions in the next dimension. You will have bodies to Infinity. You will never be without a body. It is impossible for you to conceive of yourself without a body. This foreshadows, portrays and portends that you will always have a body. Emerson says that every Spirit builds itself a house. You need a body to express the qualities of Spirit, or God.

Life Seeks Expression

The only possible motive of the All-Originating Life-Principle, which is the term used by Judge Troward for God or the Living Spirit Almighty in all of us, must be the expression of life, love, truth and beauty, which is Its nature. If man had loving thoughts and dwelled on the eternal verities, knowing and believing that his life was God's life, and really neutralized the race mind belief in death, he would not experience what the world calls physical death. Because of his meditation and prayers and because of his deep-seated conviction, the molecules of his body would oscillate at such a high frequency that he would be here, but you would not see him, no more so than you could see steam when ice is melted and heated to a certain degree. Pure steam is invisible, yet it is pure H_2O, though operating at a higher molecular frequency.

This is why, as your Bible tells you, Jesus disappeared in the crowd and could not be seen. He was able to dematerialize his body. Apollonius was able to do the same thing.

The Physical Death of the Body

The disintegrating process that you perceive is the Universal Presence and Power taking the atoms and molecules of the body for fresh construction from a tenement without a tenant, i.e., from a person who does not have the awareness or necessary faith to perpetuate the Universal Life in himself. The disintegrating force is the Integrating Power working according to the belief of the individual. It is not another power.

The Bible plus one's common sense tell us that ultimately there can be only One Power in the universe, Which must, therefore, be the Building or Creative Power. It is impossible to have a power which is negative in itself; although it shows itself negatively based on the way in which we use it or when we fail to

provide the requisite conditions for it to work positively and constructively.

Positive and Negative

This Presence and Power in you will act positively or
negatively towards you, depending upon whether you
provide positive or negative conditions for Its manifestation, in the same manner as when you may produce a positive or negative current according to the
electrical conditions which you supply. The reason for
the negative experiences in your life is your denial of
the Great Affirmative, or the practice of the Presence
of God in your life.

The higher mode of intelligence controls the lower.
God-like thoughts enthroned in your mind neutralize
and obliterate all negative thoughts. The power of the
negative in your life consists of believing that to be
true which is not true. For this reason, it is called the
father of lies in the Bible.

The Accuser

Another meaning for devil is *false accuser* or *false
affirmer*. This means the negative use of the One
Power. It means that you are going in the wrong
direction, giving the wrong instructions to your subconscious mind.

It is said that the devil has the power of death. This
is simple to perceive: Hate is the death of love, ill will
is the death of goodwill, fear is the death of faith in

God, sadness is the death of joy, pain is the death of peace, anger is the death of discernment or good judgment, ignorance is the death of truth, jealousy is the injured lover's hell, poverty is the death of God's opulence and riches, and sickness is the death of wholeness.

The Bible says: . . . *He might destroy him that had the power of death, that is, the devil; and deliver them who through fear of death were all their lifetime subject to bondage* (Hebrews 2:14–15). We are dead, Biblically speaking, when we are unaware of the Presence and Power of God within us and unaware of our capacity to use this Power righteously, thereby bringing harmony, health, peace, joy and abundance into our lives.

Satan

The word in Hebrew means *to accuse. The Guide to the Perplexed* by Maimonides, which is one of the great books of all time, points out that Satan is derived from sata, which means to slip, to err, to deviate from the truth, to turn aside or to miss the mark. The latter word is the meaning of sin. We sin when we fail to lead a full and happy life. Then we are truly sinning, as we have wandered away from the contemplation of God's Holy Presence.

When you give power to conditions, circumstances, events, or to other people to mar your happiness or thwart your good, you are giving power to externals and not to the First Cause, Which is Spirit, God, the Only Presence and Power. Giving power to externals, however, is establishing a secondary cause. A spiritual-minded person does not give power to the phenomenalistic world, which is an effect, and not a cause. He gives power to the Creator or Creative Power, not the effect. The only immaterial power you know is your thought. When your thoughts are God's thoughts, God's Power is with your thoughts of good.

Live and Evil

If you spell *live* backward, you have *evil,* which means that when we experience evil in our lives, we are living life backwards. In other words, we are going against the stream of life which could, if permitted, take us onward, upward and Godward.

The point is: Do not make an effect a cause. Nothing disturbs you except through your own thought. Where there is no opinion, there is no suffering. When you read about murder or crime in high places, you have no opinion about it. If you get exercised or agitated, who is suffering? You are. You decided to generate anger and hostility. In effect, you are generating mental poisons which are destructive to your physical organism. Where there is no judgment, there is no pain.

Cease passing judgment on people. Your judgment is the conclusion or verdict rendered in your mind. In simple language, it is your thought. Since thought is creative, whatever you think and feel about the other, you are creating in your own mind, body and experience. This is why Jesus tells you to stop judging people. *For with what judgment ye judge, ye shall be judged* . . . (Matthew 7:2).

Casting Out Devils

There are millions of people in the world and in the next dimension of life who have thoughts of hate, jealousy, hostility, greed, lust, etc. When you fill your mind with the truths of God, you neutralize and obliterate all the negative patterns. You could liken the process to pouring pure, distilled water into a bottle of dirty water. The moment comes when the last drop of dirty water is removed.

That is why it is important to keep prayed up. All of us are in the great psychic sea of over four billion people, as well as those billions living in the next dimension of life. It behooves us, therefore, to align ourselves with the Infinite Presence and Power and to constantly claim that what is true of God is true of us.

Through telepathy and thought transference, all of us are part of the great psychic sea. Subjectively, we are all one. If we are negligent, apathetic, lazy, indolent and refuse to pray, we will receive the negativity of the mass mind; and then we will say, "Why did this happen to me?"

It happened because when we fail to do our own

thinking, the race mind will do our thinking for us. When it reaches a point of saturation, it is, perhaps, precipitated as an accident, sickness or some other negative condition or tragedy. The jealous or envious person is open to all of the jealous and envious thoughts of others, because he or she is at the low level of vibration and the antenna of the mind is keyed in to that frequency, which magnifies the destructive pattern in the subconscious.

The law of attraction works for all. Like attracts like. Let us, therefore, follow the apostolic advice and conform to this spiritual injunction: *Finally, brethren, whatsoever things are true, whatsoever things are honest, whatsoever things are just, whatsoever things are pure, whatsoever things are lovely, whatsoever things are of good report; if there be any virtue, and if there be any praise, think on these things* (Philippians 4:8).

Auto-Suggestion

The conception of a devil, satan or principle of evil receives its power solely from our own auto-suggestion of its existence and because of the amenability of our subconscious to suggestion. You create what you fear. The power of evil spirits results from the mental attitude which receives such suggestions, and the subconscious responds accordingly. The suggestions of others have no power to create the things they suggest.

The Creative Power is your own thought. The antidote to all of this is the right conception of God and

His love. The Bible says, *God is love.* It also says, *. . . If God be for us, who can be against us?* (Romans 8:31). Then you realize that *. . . Perfect love casteth out fear . . .* (I John 4:18), with the result that in your mind and heart there is no devil, but God reigns supreme in your mind. It is wonderful!

I recommend that the reader read Chapter 8 (The Devil) of *Bible Mystery and Bible Meaning* by Judge Thomas Troward. In this chapter I have expatiated on some of the points on which he has dwelled.

CHAPTER 13

You Can Control Your Fears

Fear is the cause of great misery, and untold suffering and fear come to all of us. Many are afraid of the future, old age, insecurity, some illness or incurable condition, or the verdict of the doctors. Many are full of fear regarding their families, newspaper reports and the media in general, all of which project fear propaganda of all kinds. Fear of nuclear warfare, inflation and crime disturbs the masses.

Great numbers of individuals are afraid of death and loneliness in their old age. There are countless thousands who face death with equanimity and serenity, because they know that there is no death, only life, and that they will live forever in the many mansions (dimensions) of our Father's house.

There is a limitless catalogue of fears that afflict the human mind. The answer to all fear is to turn to the God-Presence within. Faith in God casts out fear. . . . *Fear hath torment. He that feareth is not made perfect in love* (I John 4:18).

YOU CAN CONTROL YOUR FEARS

You begin to think and speak in a new tongue when you turn to God within and mentally dwell on the promises of the Bible. As you continue to dwell on these great Truths, you will experience a sense of peace and security. Examine some of your fears and you will discover that many of them are groundless.

While speaking in a club here in Leisure World, a man said to me that for the greater part of his life he had been a chronic worrier. His greatest worries were those that never came to pass, but these worries depleted his vitality and brought on ulcers and high blood pressure. On the advice of a spiritual practitioner, he began to study and apply the teachings of the 23rd and 27th Psalms, which brought about a remarkable healing. He began to control and discipline his thinking. When worry thoughts came to his mind he would recite a verse or two of one of the Psalms, and in time he overcame his worries. He had discovered that all of his worries were unfounded and groundless.

Face Your Fears

There is no occasion to feel ashamed of the fact that you experience fear or that you get frightened once in awhile. The thing to do is to supplant the fear thoughts with God-like thoughts. Do not fight the fear in your mind; proceed at once to overcome it. You can do it, and it does not call for superhuman effort, only a redirection of your thought-life.

213

HOW TO USE THE LAWS OF MIND

The Secret Place

He that dwelleth in the secret place of the most High shall abide under the shadow of the Almighty (Psalm 91:1). The secret place is your own mind. Turn within and realize that the Presence of God indwells you. You can communicate with this Divine Presence through your thought, and a definite response will come.

The word *shadow* means protection, somewhat similar to a woman's use of an umbrella to protect herself from the penetrating rays of the sun. When fear thoughts come to you, repeat a few verses of the 91st Psalm many, many times. Do this quietly, feelingly and knowingly, and you will discover that a sense of peace and security will come quietly and gently into your mind and heart. When your mind is at peace, you are in the secret place, for God is absolute peace and harmony.

Fear may come to your mind again and again because of habit; but persist in supplanting the fear thoughts with a few verses of the 91st Psalm, such as the first and second verses, and you will find that you will gradually become the master of your fears. Every time you enthrone constructive thoughts, such as "God's love fills my mind and heart" or "God's peace fills my soul," you are wiping out your fear and strengthening your faith and confidence in God and His love. Your abnormal fear will then gradually diminish and vanish.

YOU CAN CONTROL YOUR FEARS

Bible Techniques

There are marvelous texts in the Bible for overcoming fear. Become a habitual peruser of the 91st, 27th, 46th and 23rd Psalms,* and you will gradually saturate your subconscious with the eternal verities and be free. The following verse will work wonders in your life: *There is no fear in love; but perfect love casteth out fear; because fear hath torment. He that feareth is not made perfect in love* (I John 4:18).

Love is an emotional attachment. It is an outpouring of goodwill. Spiritually, it means that you recognize the Presence of God in all His creatures. A woman who was terrified of dogs (probably dating back to her childhood when she was bitten by a dog, since she had a faint memory of the incident) began to affirm: "I radiate love to all dogs. They love their masters and they save lives. The Presence of God is in all of his creatures. I love dogs. They are loving, kind and cooperative."

She kept affirming these truths and after a period of time she was at peace with dogs. She no longer feared them. You will lose fear as you grow in understanding that there is only One Power.

Dwell also on these wonderful words: *The Lord is my light and my salvation; whom shall I fear? the Lord is the strength of my life; of whom shall I be afraid?* (Psalm 27:1).

*See *Songs of God* by Dr. Joseph Murphy, DeVorss and Company, Inc., Marina del Rey, California, 1979.

215

When fearful, reiterate these truths over and over again, and you will sense an inner peace and security. In the Bible it also says: *Fear not, for I am with thee . . .* (Isaiah 43:5). *He shall not be afraid of evil tidings: his heart is fixed, trusting in the Lord* (Psalm 112:7). *Fear thou not; for I am with thee: be not dismayed; for I am thy God: I will strengthen thee; yea, I will help thee; yea, I will uphold thee with the right hand of my righteousness. For I the Lord thy God will hold thy right hand, saying unto thee, Fear not; I will help thee* (Isaiah 41:10,13).

Select some of these verses or all of them and recite them slowly, quietly and reverently, knowing that as you repeat these truths, they will sink down into your subconscious mind, eradicating and neutralizing all of the fear patterns. You will feel strengthened and enlightened.

A Bible Verse Saved Her Estate

A woman who was being sued falsely by some of her relatives over an estate adhered to this Truth: . . . *In God I have put my trust; I will not fear what flesh can do unto me* (Psalm 56:4). She did not waver in her faith, and the case was dismissed.

Take refuge in the great Psalms. As you enthrone these Truths in your mind, you will discover that your fears will subside and give way to a sense of peace and security.

YOU CAN CONTROL YOUR FEARS

Who Is Your Lord?

For in the time of trouble he shall hide me in his pavilion: in the secret of his tabernacle shall he hide me: he shall set me up upon a rock (Psalm 27:5).

Who is your Lord and master this very moment? Your Lord is your predominant mental attitude; it is your conviction or belief about yourself, people and things. This Lord can be a tyrant. For example, if your mood is now one of resentment, that is your Lord or tyrant that governs all of your actions and all phases of your life. If you want to invest some money, buy a new home or buy some property while in this attitude, you will do and say the wrong thing because your predominant mood is negative. The law is: "As within, so without." You are fearing your good, and you would react negatively. Fear is a lack of faith or trust in God, which is a denial of His Omnipotence.

The Lord is my light and my salvation . . . (Psalm 27:1). *The Lord* referred to is the Lord God, or the law of God or good. To put the law of good into operation —thereby banishing fear once and for all—enthrone in your mind the thoughts of power, courage and confidence. These thoughts will generate a corresponding mood or feeling, which will banish the arch enemy of your success and health.

Fear, this self-made enemy of yours, must be completely destroyed before the Lord God can shine

217

through you. Your fear is the cloud that hides the sunshine of God. Men have made personal devils out of fear of the past, the present and the future.

It is our attitude toward life that determines the experience we are to meet. If we expect misfortune, we shall have it. Knowing the law of God or good, the truth student expects only good fortune. The world is not harsh; it may seem to be, because we fail to affirm or claim the Presence of God. Men fear criticism so much that many of their most beautiful thoughts never see the light of day. To the man who believes that God is the only Presence and the only Power, there is no past; he knows that if he believes in the power of the past, he is disbelieving in God. God is the Eternal Now; there is no future and no past in God.

This is the Gospel—the good tidings. There is no such thing as past karma; there is only man's foolish, false belief in it. . . . *Now is the day of salvation* (II Corinthians 6:2). The Kingdom of Heaven is at hand. Your good, your health and your success are here now; feel the reality of them; thrill to them. Enter into the conviction that you are now the being you long to be.

Guilt and What It Means

The only guilt there is is the consciousness of guilt. . . . *Though your sins be as scarlet, they shall be as*

218

white as snow; though they be red like crimson, they shall be as wool (Isaiah 1:18). This is the good news. The only moment that matters is the present. You can live only in the now, experience in the now, plan in the now and think in the now. Whatever you are planning or dreading, you are planning it now. When you realize that every form of lack and limitation is the result of your wrong thinking and feeling, you shall know the Truth that sets you free. The mountains will be removed.

Aboriginal tribes and primitive man feared nature. Modern man fears his fellow man. To a great extent we have dispelled the ghosts of ancient days. We have combatted the plagues, and we will soon control the elements. Man is doped by modern propaganda. Some men are afraid to live and afraid to speak. Mothers fear for their children. All this is due to superstitious belief that there is another power to challenge God.

The only evil there is is due to a lack of knowledge of the laws of life. If we put our hand on an open wire we get a shock, but if it is insulated properly we do not. The evil or shock was due to our ignorance; yet any man will admit that electricity is not evil. It blesses man in countless ways. Electricity is used to play music, drive trains, fry eggs, vacuum the floors and light the world. Evil or fear is our misapplication and incomplete comprehension of the Omnipresence of God, or good. Where fear is, love cannot be; for error cannot dwell with understanding.

The wealthy fear they are going to lose; the poor fear they will not gain. The only wealth and the only security are found in the consciousness in which we abide. If we are conscious of being wealthy, nothing in all the world can stop us from being prosperous in our bodies and affairs. The things men fear are unreal. Only the One alone is real; only the One alone is Law; only the One alone is Truth.

The jungle doctor of old has passed on many of his superstitions; consequently, countless cults today instill fear into the minds of many individuals. Let us face the facts. The cause of most fear is man's fear of his fellow man. Many men pray together on Sunday and prey on each other on Monday.

The answer to the fear problem is understanding. All fear is due to ignorance. In order to express harmony, we must think and feel harmonious thoughts. When we enter into the mood of success, confidence and happiness, we will express similar results in all phases of our life. When man knows that every form of discord, sickness and lack is due to wrong thinking, he will know the Truth which sets him free.

Use Your Imagination

Learn to imagine the thing desired, then feel the reality of the state sought. This is the easiest and quickest way to get results. Some get results by convincing themselves of the Truth that God is the only Presence and the only Power. This is one of the most wonderful things in all of the world to know.

Regardless of the cause of the fear, you have no one to treat or heal but yourself. You have to convince yourself that you are now expressing life, love and truth. Let us not fear anything or anybody; let us be busy radiating courage, confidence and power. In this way we will crush all obstacles in our path, and the mountains will be cast into the sea.

We are one with Infinite Power. If we say we are weak or infirm, we are telling a falsehood about God. Fear turns the love of God or good away from us in the same way that a poverty consciousness attracts poverty in health, money, business and love relationships. Man must stop preaching fear to his fellow man and unite in teaching all of the Truth.

God Is Timeless and Spaceless

The Truth is that there is no hell, devil, purgatory, limbo or damnation of any kind; moreover, there is no past karma for which we must expiate here and there is no future evil. God is the Eternal Now! This is one of the most dramatic and significant statements in the whole Bible: . . . *Now is the day of salvation* (II Corinthians 6:2). This very moment all that you need to do is to turn to God and claim for yourself that which you long to be. Accept it; believe it, and go thy way rejoicing. . . . *Though your sins be as scarlet, they shall be as white as snow; though they be red like crimson, they shall be as wool* (Isaiah 1:18). . . . (Forgive) *Until seventy times seven* (Matthew 18:22). . . . *To day shalt thou be with me in paradise* (Luke 23:43).

Let us stop instilling fear into the minds of the youth; let us teach them the real facts. We must not preach religious tolerance unless we live it. We must teach the Truth. We must not distort the Truth so that we may hold a position or because we are afraid that the people will not come back. This type of fear results in spiritual stagnation and frustration. We must keep our eye on the Kingdom of Heaven, not upon the kingdom of earth. We must teach man to know the Truth, and the Truth shall make him free. The Truth is: Man is belief expressed!

There is no fear where faith in God rules. There is no fear of man where integrity rules in one's consciousness. There is no fear of criticism where the consciousness of kindliness enters into the mind of man. Religion is goodwill in action or the application of the golden rule. We have seen, therefore, that fear is man's basic weakness, and it is based solely on ignorance.

. . . *In the time of trouble he shall hide me in his pavilion: in the secret of his tabernacle shall he hide me; he shall set me up upon a rock* (Psalm 27:5). The *pavilion* is a canopy or covering; this means the covering shall be the garment of God (mood of good). Think about God. Begin to ask yourself, "What does God mean to me?" Realize that God, or I AM, is the life in you, your own consciousness, and It is Omnipotent.

God and Good Are Synonymous

For example, if a man is in prison, he automatically desires freedom. God and good are synonymous. He begins to think of this Infinite Power and Wisdom within him. He knows that It has ways of freeing him of which he has no knowledge. He imagines, therefore, the opposite, which is freedom. Though he is behind bars, in meditation he imagines that he is at home talking to his loved ones. He hears familiar voices and feels the welcoming kisses of his children on his cheek. This is hiding in the *pavilion*. The prisoner actualizes this state by feeling the joy of being home. It is possible to rise high enough in consciousness in five or ten minutes to bring about a subjective conviction. This is the meaning of . . . *In the secret of his tabernacle shall he hide me* . . . (Psalm 27:5). The law is: Whatever is impressed is expressed; consequently, the prison doors are open for him in ways of which he has no knowledge. . . . *His ways are past finding out* (Romans 11:33).

We read in the Scriptures: *Fear not, little flock; for it is your Father's good pleasure to give you the kingdom* (Luke 12:32). Jesus tells us this Kingdom is within us—this Kingdom of Heaven or harmony is within every one of us. Infinite Wisdom, Divine Intelligence and Infinite Power are available to all men, because God is within them and He is the very life of them. Anyone can prove to himself that the Kingdom of Heaven is at hand. It is right here now. Jesus saw it and lived in it. We are color blind; that is why we do not see it. The blindness is due to ignorance and fear. We are blinded by centuries of false beliefs, superstition, creeds and dogmas. The Truth is so shrouded by false dogmas that we have created God and a heaven of our making. God is to us what we believe Him to be. Man has created a horrendous creature in the skies. He visualizes a God of caprice and vengeance, or an inscrutable being who sends wars, plagues, etc. We create our own hell and our own heaven, based upon our concept of God. Anyone can prove that the Kingdom of Heaven is at hand.

Prayer Casts Out Fear

Let me tell you the story of a young girl who proved it. She was living with a father who came home drunk every night and who sometimes treated her brutally. She lived in constant fear of her father. She kept house for him. Due to frustration, her face was covered with acne.

224

We are not living with people; we are living with our concept of them. Realizing this truth, the girl closed her eyes in meditation and dwelt on the God Power within her. She no longer clothed her father in the garment or mood of a drunkard. Instead, she saw a loving, kind father, who had perfect balance, poise and equilibrium. She clothed him in righteousness, and her . . . *judgment was a robe and a diadem* (Job 29:14), which means that she saw her father as he ought to be. The fact that her father was drinking heavily meant that he was seeking to escape to conceal an inferiority complex or a subjective sense of loss. In other words, he was trying to run away from himself.

This girl spoke the word which healed him. She relaxed her whole body, closed her eyes and began to say to herself, "How would I feel if my father were loving, kind and peaceful?" She dwelt on the solution, which generated a mood of peace, confidence and joy within her. This was clothing him in righteousness. Her judgment was a *robe and diadem*.

When you pass judgment, you come to a decision. It is the final verdict, and you are the judge passing judgment. . . . *As I hear, I judge . . .* (John 5:30). Her verdict was an inner hearing or feeling, wherein she saw her father smiling, happy and joyous. She imagined he was telling her how wonderful he felt and that he had found peace, balance and poise. She also heard him telling her how wonderful she was. She thrilled to the fact that her father was healed and made whole. *He wore a seamless robe*—no holes, no patches and no seams. This means that she meditated on the mood of love, peace and oneness with her ideal. All doubts and fears were absent, which means *judgment as the robe. Judgment as the diadem* means that she gave *beauty for ashes,* which signifies that she saw beauty in her father and felt it.

After one week's treatment, her father was completely healed; moreover, he was a changed man. His attitude was completely transformed, and he and his daughter are now devoted to each other. She proved the Kingdom of Heaven (harmony and peace) is at hand NOW. What are we afraid of? *If God be for us, who can be against us?* (Romans 8:31). The thing you fear does not exist.

For example, a man might live in fear that his business will fail. His business is not failing; neither is he in bankruptcy. Business is as usual, and it may be booming. The failure does not exist except in his imagination. Job said, . . . *the thing which I greatly feared is come upon me* . . . (Job 3:25). Job is every man who walks the earth. Therefore, as the successful businessman continues to sustain the mood of failure, sooner or later his mood crystallizes into a subjective conviction or impression.

Any feeling impressed on the subconscious mind is made manifest by an immutable law of life. The subconscious, being impersonal and no respecter of persons, says, "John wants to fail in business," so it proceeds in ways that he (John) knows not of to bring this failure to pass. Everyone realizes that he brought this failure on himself through imagination and feeling.

Let Divine Love Go Before You

I knew a lady who read of an airplane wreck. She was contemplating a trip by air to Los Angeles, but she lived in fear of an accident. A negative thought cannot do you any harm unless it is energized by a charge of fear. It must be emotionalized before it becomes subjective. This lady did not know what she was doing; she was ignorant of the laws of life. This ignorance is the cause of all of our accidents and misfortunes. Having imagined herself in an airplane accident and having emotionalized this negative thought with fear, it became a subjective state. When she took the trip two months later, she had the accident that she "knew" she would have.

If a woman fears that her husband is going to leave her, this is how she conquers her moods. The fear is a negative feeling which is communicated to him. If he does not know the laws of life, her conviction of him will be made manifest. In other words, he will do the thing she feared he would do, because this was her conviction of him. Instead of this fear, she supplants it by seeing her husband radiating peace, health and happiness. In meditation morning and night, she radiates the mood of love and peace and feels that her husband is the most wonderful man in all the world. She feels that he is loving, kind and devoted. She imagines he is telling her how wonderful she is and how happy, free and balanced he is. Her mood of fear is now changed to a mood of love and peace. This is the Spirit of God moving in her behalf. As she continues to do this, this mood gels within her. She now knows, *He never faileth* (Zephaniah 3:5), and that *. . . perfect love casteth out fear . . .* (I John 4:18).

Our daily prayer or daily mood must be one of joyous expectancy or a confident expectancy of all good things. This is our greatest prayer. If we expect the best, the best will come to us. It is our mood that is vital.

The modern metaphysician teaches that God is the life principle within man. If you feel full of confidence and trust, this is the movement of the Spirit of God within you, and It is all powerful. . . . *None can stay his hand, or say unto him, What doest thou?* (Daniel 4:35). Man's own consciousness is God; there is no other God. By consciousness is meant existence, life and awareness.

You, the reader, know that you exist. This knowing that you exist is God. What you are aware of is your concept of God. Each man must ask himself, "What am I aware of?" The answer to this question is his belief about God. It is what he knows about God. When he says, "I am aware of want, I am fearful, I am sick," these are lies and have no truth in them. When man says, "I am fearful," he is saying that God is full of fear, which is nonsensical. When he says, "I am in want," he is relating a lie and a denial of God's abundance and infinite supply. His faith is in failure, and he succeeds in being a failure. He believes in a lie, but he cannot prove the lie. The false condition seems real as long as he dwells upon it. When he ceases to believe it, he is free and healed.

CHAPTER 14

The Power of Suggestion

You have heard the Biblical expression, . . . *Thy faith hath made thee whole* . . . (Mark 5:34). The obvious meaning is that the power which effects the healing is resident within the individual and not in any extraneous form. Jesus proclaimed faith as the one prepotent agency in the healing process. Faith is the mental attitude of the individual which releases the spiritual agencies within all of us. Many methods of healing prevail in the world today. They are varied in the many countries of the world. The only prerequisite to all of these methods is the requisite confidence on the part of the patient, then results follow.

The Bible tells us that Jesus could not do many wonderful works among the people of his village because of their unbelief. In order for you to get positive results, it is necessary that you understand the principles involved.

There are two phases of your mind, commonly referred to as objective mind and subjective mind, or you can use the terms conscious and subconscious minds. Many refer to these two phases of your mind as the supraliminal and the subliminal. The conscious, or objective mind is the mind of ordinary waking consciousness, which takes cognizance of the objective world by means of the five senses, whereas the subconscious mind* is the builder of the body and manifests itself in all subjective states and conditions, as in hypnotism, sleep, clairvoyance, clairaudience, somnambulism, trance, dreams, etc., when the conscious mind is asleep or wholly or partially subjugated. Your subconscious is always active; it never sleeps.

How Suggestion Works

You must remember that your subconscious mind is constantly amenable to control by the power of suggestion. There is a clear line of differentiation between the two phases of your mind both as to their powers and to their limitations. One of the corollaries of the law of suggestion is that your subconscious mind is incapable of inductive reasoning, which means that it is not capable of conducting independently a line of research by collecting facts, classifying them and estimating their relative evidential values.

Your subconscious accepts whatever suggestions

*See *The Power of Your Subconscious Mind* by Dr. Joseph Murphy, Prentice-Hall, Inc., Englewood Cliffs, N.J., 1963.

are imparted to it, whether these suggestions are false or true. Its method of reasoning is purely deductive, and its power of deduction seems to be well nigh perfect. Remember, all this is true whether the premise be true or false. That is to say, your subconscious mind deductions from a false premise are as logically correct as from a true one. This is why it is extremely important what you suggest to your subconscious mind.

Your Auto-Suggestion

Remember, an auto-suggestion is just as potent, other things being equal, as a suggestion from another person. When your subconscious is confronted with two opposing suggestions, the stronger one necessarily prevails. You can reject all negative suggestions given to you, and at the same time, you can contemplate the One Power—the Power of God—functioning and operating in you, thereby neutralizing any negative suggestions given to you.

The Wonders of Your Deeper Mind

Your whole body is made up of a confederation of intelligent cells, each of which performs its functions with an amazing intelligence according to its special duties. Your body is composed of billions of cells, and your body does not rest when you are asleep —that is an illusion. Your heart beats, you breathe regularly, digestion and assimilation go on cease-lessly, circulation of blood continues, the body per-spires, hair grows, finger nails grow, etc. You might say that your body slows down, but, actually, it does not rest.

It is your conscious mind that rests as you withdraw from the vexations, strife, contentions and anxieties of the day. In sleep, the conscious mind is cut off and the wisdom and intelligence of your subconscious takes over. The healing process takes place when you are asleep. This is why you read in the 23rd Psalm: *He restoreth my soul. . . . He giveth his beloved sleep* (Psalm 127:2).

She Visited a Kahuna

A woman residing in Leisure World told me that about ten years ago she suffered from what had been called an incurable malady. She decided to see a kahuna, who is a native priest in the Hawaiian Is-lands. She said that he went into a certain ritual of prayer, including native incantations, which she did not understand. After a half an hour or so, he told her that she should repeat "God is" over and over again at night as she goes to sleep and that she would be healed.

She said that his attitude was so impressive that she was convinced a healing would follow. So, when she had awakened the next morning, she knew instinctively and intuitively that she was healed. All subsequent tests verified her inner knowing.

This demonstrates the power of faith, or a complete mental acceptance on her part, which released the Infinite Healing Presence within her, making her whole and perfect. This silent partner in all of us is all-wise. You can call It God, if you like, or the Superconscious, the I AM, the Christ within, subconscious wisdom and intelligence or the Higher-Self. The point is that this power and wisdom is within each of us, and it is our God-given privilege to contact this Super Intelligence and apply It. The Bible says, *Acquaint now thyself with him, and be at peace . . .* (Job 22:21).

Healers

There are mental, psychic and spiritual healing agencies, churches and individuals all over the world. Many of them seek to prove that only their method is correct. This is obviously not true, as all of them get healings. The Blackfoot Indian medicine man and the witchdoctor in Africa get healings, also.

There is one universal Healing Presence available to all. The method of healing is faith, whether blind faith or true faith. The latter is based on the knowledge of the working of your deeper mind. We might reflect here and realize that for untold ages, suggestion was the only therapeutic agency available to man. Medicine, if we look upon its advent from

Hippocrates, called "the father of medicine," who practiced about 400 B.C., is a vast, modern institution today when compared with that long line of healers through the centuries who had marvelous healings through the power of suggestion in its countless forms.

Any form of belief which inspires the faith of the patient, when supplemented by a corresponding healing suggestion, is definitely efficacious. You might say that anything the patient has faith in is efficacious as healing therapy.

The Fetish Worshipper

There are fetish worshippers who believe that a carving of wood or bone possesses magical powers or is endowed with energies or qualities capable of bringing about a healing or protection according to the design of the owner. The fetish sometimes is believed to be the abode of a supernatural power and gains its potency from the indwelling of that spirit.

Many ill people throughout the world invoke the aid of these sticks, trees or bones, supposedly inhabited by spirits; and during the performance of the rites by the medicine man, they are restored to health. Why? It is because the ceremony or ritual constitutes a powerful suggestion which activates the healing power resident in the subconscious mind. Furthermore, the ceremony inspires faith and receptivity, releasing the Infinite Intelligence which controls the body.

North American Indian Healings

Some of the North American Indians believe that evil spirits cause all disease. His medicine man tells the sick man that he can frighten and expel the evil spirits by incantation, gyrations of his body, frightful noises, etc., supplemented by a weird, grotesque makeup. The patient is highly suggestible and, of course, very receptive, and the evil spirits flee in a short period of time, leaving the sick man to recover. It is foolish to say that they don't have healings. However, it is all based on suggestions: nothing more, nothing less.

One highly educated Indian who was a medical doctor told me that to the untutored and unlettered mind of the poor Indians, this method of healing is ofttimes more effective than the material remedies of the highly up-to-date and modern physician. All healing agencies are effective in exact proportion to their faith-inspiring potency.

It is not surprising, therefore, that in the days of primitive humanity, when superstition and ignorance were universal, there prevailed countless methods of healing therapies. It is foolish to scoff at the primitive beliefs and practices in vogue when humanity was in its infancy. God's universal healing presence is available to all. God, in His infinite mercy, had instituted a subconscious law adapted to the belief of every level of human intelligence. All healing methods are adapted to some special grade of intelligence.

Truth Is Eternal

Nothing is permanent but Truth. Error loses its vitality in the sunlight of Truth; hence, all institutions that are based on fundamental error cannot permanently endure in the presence of fundamental Truth. Wrong systems and techniques may endure for a long time, but their good effects become less and less in evidence and so they finally vanish.

Action and reaction are always equal. Hence, when a student of Truth learns the basis of all these forms of healing, he knows there is only one Healing Presence which responds to his call upon It and that It responds to all. Then he gives up all the popular but erroneous systems of healing because he knows the Truth and the way the mind works. The Truth student is no longer looking for some extraneous intelligence; rather, he looks inside of himself and realizes that he can control the workings of his subconscious mind, which, in turn, controls all vital functions. The Truth student's faith is based on a knowledge of the laws of mind, not of blind credulity.

Overcoming Alcoholism

It is impossible for one to suggest universal principles to another without being benefited himself. For example, some professional hypnotists have told me that when they make suggestions to the alcoholic, they are healed of alcoholism themselves. In other words, they said that it is impossible for one to be a drunkard when he is employing suggestions for the eradication of drinking habits in the patient. One hypnotist stated that he was unable to bear the smell or taste of liquor after making a series of affirmations and vigorous suggestions to an alcoholic that the taste and smell of liquor would thereafter make him sick.

The law of mind is that an auto-suggestion is as effective as a suggestion from another. The conscious mind suggests and the subconscious mind accepts and believes the suggestion, performing its function accordingly.

Many people use auto-suggestion for the eradication of smoking, excessive drinking and other bad habits. In other words, anyone can relieve himself of any habit he *sincerely desires* to get rid of. It often happens that the alcoholic goes to a specialist, but in his heart he has no real desire to be free from the habit. This creates an adverse auto-suggestion which necessarily defeats the operator or specialist.

Remember, a very important point is to know that all suggestions to a patient react upon the one who makes the suggestion. Action and reaction are always equal. The principle is as true of mental as well as physical energy. It is like the quality of mercy: "It is twice blessed; it blesseth him that gives and him that takes."

Darwin's Comments

In the *Descent of Man,* Darwin points out that intelligent actions by animals, after being performed during several generations, become converted into instincts and are inherited, as when birds on the oceanic islands avoid man. His reference to the birds on the oceanic islands is very interesting, pointing out the way the subjective minds of animals and birds act. When man first visited those hitherto uninhabited islands, he noticed that the birds were completely void of fear of the biped who walked among them, but they soon learned their lesson—that he was armed with a weapon that was fatal to them. This was communicated subjectively to their offspring, and whenever man appeared after that, they flew away. Some hunters tell us that they very soon learned to measure with great accuracy the effective range of man's guns. Gradually, during several generations, the fear of man was converted into an inheritable instinct. Thereafter, the youngest bird was as fearful of his enemy—man—as was his experienced ancestors.

Control of Animals

Were it not for the law of suggestion, it would be impossible for man to tame a tiger, subdue an elephant or tame a wild horse. The horse is subjective and subject to the conscious control of man. In order to be subject to man, the horse must be made to believe that man is much stronger than a horse. The horse trainer usually accomplishes this feat by throwing the animal and holding him down until he ceases to struggle. Man can bind his legs with a rope. When man has successfully accomplished his superiority, the rest is easy, for man's suggestion of superior strength has been communicated to the subjective mind of the horse that it is useless to struggle against such power. The subconscious mind of the horse is amenable to suggestion and control by the conscious mind of man.

The principle prevails in all encounters between man and the lower animals. Just in proportion to man's success in imparting suggestions to the animal he seeks to subdue will he succeed in rendering the animal permanently obedient and docile. Man is enabled to assert and maintain his dominion over the animal creation by virtue of the law of suggestion.

She Had a Remarkable Recovery

While speaking in Atlanta, Georgia, some months ago, a woman came to see me. During the course of the conversation, she said that a year previously two bandits had come into her store and had told her to open the safe and to hurry up. She was on crutches and she protested, pointing out that her husband would be there in a few minutes and that he usually opened the safe, because she had great difficulty bending down. One of the bandits then pointed a gun at her head and said, "I will give you thirty seconds to open the safe; if not, I will blow your head off." She threw away her crutches and opened the safe. She never used the crutches after that.

Self-preservation is the first law of nature—the idea to save her life at all costs seized her mind and all the power of the Infinite flowed to that focal point of attention, bringing forth a remarkable healing. The power of God, or the Infinite Healing Presence, was within her all the time, but she had never called upon It, so It remained dormant. The Living Spirit Almighty was within her, as It is within all people. It cannot be paralyzed or crippled; and in the presence of that great shock, she forgot she was crippled and released the power that moves the world.

Paralytics Walk and Run

The late Dr. Frederick Bailes told me that a number of helpless paralytics were confined to a hospital in South America and that somehow a boa constrictor had crawled into the ward through an open window. All the paralytics ran out of the ward into the yard outside, and all had become completely healed.

The Annals of Medicine

Many physicians in the United States and other countries have reported in medical journals extraordinary feats of strength, so-called miraculous healings taking place in the presence of a great shock such as fire in the home, a sudden catastrophe or a great emergency. The following article appeared in the *National Enquirer* January 29, 1980:

> ### Tiny Housewife Lifts 4,500-Pound Car to Free Child Pinned Under a Wheel
>
> In a rush of superhuman strength, a 118-pound woman lifted a 4,600-pound Cadillac with her bare hands to free an 8-year-old girl pinned under the front wheel.
>
> "All I can think is that God gave me the strength," says 44-year-old Martha Weiss, who stands 5 feet 3 inches.
>
> Now, children are calling her "Wonder Woman," and the police have given her a hero's citation.
>
> The gut-wrenching drama unfolded when Mrs. Weiss saw the car hit little Berta Amaral in front of Our Lady of Mount Carmel in San Diego, drag her 20 feet and stop on top of her.
>
> "Everyone seemed to freeze in horror," recalled Mrs. Weiss, who had just dropped off her own children at the school.

"The little girl's mother was crawling under the car trying to reach her.

"All I could think of was that woman's desperation as she tried to pull her daughter out.

"I knew I had to do something. I ran over and grabbed the front side of the car.

"The girl was under the right front wheel. She couldn't breathe. I said a silent prayer and strained with all my might. I could feel the metal cutting into my fingers—but the car didn't move an inch.

"I looked down at the pitiful face lying under the car, and I knew I had to lift it off of her.

"I tried again and, at first, nothing happened. Then suddenly I felt a new strength rush into my body. It was as though an invisible hand was suddenly helping me—and the car started to lift. I couldn't believe that it was actually happening, but then I screamed at the girl's mother to pull her free.

"As her tiny body came free of the car, I suddenly felt its full weight cutting into my fingers again and I had to let it drop."

Young Berta was rushed to a nearby hospital following the December 6 accident and is now recovering.

San Diego Policeman Bill Robinson, who

investigated the accident which earned Mrs. Weiss an official recommendation, told *The Enquirer:*

"The car weighed about 2½ tons—and she did lift the full weight of the front end off the child. I've heard of men managing to do something like this, with a rush of adrenaline, but never a woman. It's really amazing."

A Cadillac spokeswoman said the car, a 1968 Coupe De Ville, weighed 4,595 pounds. The driver was cited for reckless driving.

Reflecting on her accomplishment, Mrs. Weiss said: "I simply did it because it had to be done. My children are telling everyone that their mother is 'Wonder Woman'—but God must have worked through me that day."

—Malcolm Boyes

The late Henry Hamblin, Editor of the *Science of Thought Review,* Chichester, England, told me of a man who had lived a short distance from him. He was completely paralyzed due to polio and could move only rather slowly with two crutches. His two boys, ages six and seven, had been in the next room when the house caught on fire. He had rushed in and raised his two boys on his shoulders and run down the stairs. He had run into the street and asked a neighbor to call the fire brigade. He had walked for years after that incident, completely cured. The idea to save the lives of both of his little boys had seized his mind, and the power of the Almighty had moved on his behalf and he had responded accordingly. Love conquers all.

Husband Has Morning Sickness

Recently I counselled with a man who had suffered with his wife the pangs of what he called "morning sickness" during her pregnancy. I sent him to a doctor friend of mine, who could find nothing physically wrong with him. This is not a strange phenomenon; it was due to his subconscious rapport with his wife. The constant telepathic communication brought on the same symptoms. It could be called psychological sympathy between husband and wife.

I gave him the following prayer to use three or four times a day:

> *Thou wilt keep him in perfect peace, whose mind is stayed on thee: because he trusteth in thee* (Isaiah 26:3). I know that the inner desires of my heart come from God within me. God wants me to be happy. The will of God for me is life, love, truth, and beauty. I mentally accept my good now and I become a perfect channel for the Divine.
>
> I come into His Presence singing; I enter into His courts with praise; I am joyful and happy; I am still and poised.

The Still Small Voice whispers in my ear revealing to me my perfect answer. I am an expression of God. I am always in my true place doing the thing I love to do. I refuse to accept the opinions of man as truth. I now turn within and I sense and feel the rhythm of the Divine. I hear the melody of God whispering its message of love to me.

My mind is God's mind, and I am always reflecting Divine wisdom and Divine intelligence. My brain symbolizes my capacity to think wisely and spiritually. God's ideas unfold within my mind with perfect sequence. I am always poised, balanced, serene and calm, for I know that God will always reveal to me the perfect solution to all my needs.

Whenever I think of my wife I will affirm immediately, "God's peace fills your soul. God loves you and cares for you."

Following this procedure, he became completely free from all symptoms.

CHAPTER 15

Marriage, Sex, and Divorce

In Munich a woman asked me: "What about the relationship between faith and works?" This is a very practical question. It is said that . . . *faith, if it hath not works, is dead* . . . (James 2:17). The faith spoken of in the Bible, however, has nothing whatever to do with faith in a creed, such as the Jewish, Catholic, Protestant or Buddhist faith. It means faith in the Creative Law of the Universe, faith that whatever is impressed on the subconscious mind will be experienced.

Faith, Biblically speaking, has nothing to do with any religious persuasion. Have faith that every thought is creative. What you feel and imagine to be true will come to pass, whether good or bad. Your real faith is the silent inner knowing of your own soul; it is your inner, practical, functioning belief regarding God, life and your fellow man. It is the real belief of your heart that is made manifest, not what you superficially give intellectual assent to. The Book of Proverbs says: *For as he thinketh in his heart, so is*

247

he (Proverbs 23:7). That is your real faith and your real religion.

Dr. Erhard Freitag, Leopoldstrasse Be 70, 8000 Munich 40, West Germany, has invited me several times to give lectures in Germany and Switzerland. He is an outstanding spiritual psychologist, a Doctor of Divine Science, and a marvelous lecturer and teacher of the powers of your subconscious mind. His associate, Professor Manfred G. Schmidt, has translated many of my books into the German language, and he, too, is a wonderful metaphysician and lecturer. His translations of metaphysical books are superb, because he conveys intuitively and spiritually the real meaning of the author.

It was under Dr. Freitag's auspices that I have lectured in Frankfurt and Munich, Germany; Vienna, Austria; and Zurich, Switzerland, and I have experienced a wonderful response in the various cities I have visited. There is a deep spiritual renaissance in Germany and Switzerland, and I found a great hunger and thirst for the eternal verities. Many of my books have been translated into the German language, and eventually all of thirty-five books will be available in that language.

Girl in Wheel Chair Walks

Professor Schmidt introduced me to a girl who had been forced to be in a wheel chair for several years but who now walks. She had listened to lectures by Dr.

Freitag and she diligently studied *The Power of Your Subconscious Mind,* * applying the techniques outlined therein. She claimed that the Supreme Intelligence Which created her could and would heal her, and she also pictured herself doing all the things she would do were she whole and perfect. She literally lived the role in her mind and she discovered that thought upon thought, mental picture upon picture, when repeated, and feeling the reality of it all, penetrated her subconscious mind and was objectified on the screen of space.

Why She Did Not Help Her Mother

A young woman had a conference with me in Vienna, Austria. She said that she had been praying for her mother, who was in a hospital for a heart condition, but that her mother got worse. In our conversation, however, I discovered that her mind was full of the acute and dangerous symptoms and not with the power of God. Her prayers tended to magnify the trouble rather than to remove the condition. Real prayer consists of thinking of God, but she was thinking more of the infirmities, thereby perpetuating the disabilities instead of giving her mother a spiritual transfusion.

I suggested to her that she pray as follows: "My

*See *The Power of Your Subconscious Mind* by Dr. Joseph Murphy, Prentice-Hall, Inc., Englewood Cliffs, N.J., 1963.

mother is known in Divine Mind. God is, and His Healing Presence flows through her as peace, harmony, wholeness, beauty and Divine love. God loves her and cares for her. I feel and know that there is only One Healing Presence and Power and its corollary: There is no power to challenge the action of God. I claim that the vitality, intelligence and power of the Infinite are now being externalized in her whole being. I give thanks for the healing that is now taking place. I surrender her to God. Later on when I pray, I will pray as if I had never prayed before. Each time I do this, I am reinforcing the idea of wholeness and vitality, which penetrates the subconscious of my mother, and a healing follows."

She followed this spiritual prescription, and I subsequently received a wonderful letter from her stating that her mother had returned home and is now vital, strong and doing all the things she loves to do.

What to Do When You Pray

If you pray for a pathological heart or lung condition, do not think of the organ as diseased, as this would not be spiritual thinking. Thoughts are things. Your spiritual thought takes the form of cells, tissues, nerves and organs. To think of a damaged or diseased heart or of high blood pressure tends to suggest more of what you already have.

Cease dwelling on symptoms, organs or any other part of the body. Turn your mind to God and His love. Feel and know that the healing power of God is flowing through the other person. Picture the person for whom you are praying as vital, alive, and bubbling over with enthusiasm. Hear the sick person telling you about the miracle of God which has happened in his or her life. Do this as often as you are led to do it, and wonderful results will follow.

You Must Want to Be Healed

In Munich I had a consultation with a woman who suffered from arthritis. She was taking aspirin and codeine, hot baths, heat therapy, etc., but, according to her, the arthritis was getting worse.

I explained to her that the word "itis" indicates inflammation of the mind. In other words, there must exist some poison pocket in her subconscious mind, such as deep-seated resentment, hostility or an unwillingness to forgive. She admitted that she had stolen large sums of money over a period of time from her mother, who had previously passed on to the next dimension of life, and she felt very guilty and believed that she should be punished, thereby causing this inflammatory condition of her body.

Ofttimes, the explanation is the cure. I asked her if she would steal now. She replied, "No. I am leading a good, honest life." Then I reminded her that she was not the same woman spiritually, mentally or physically who had formerly stolen the money. I said to her, "You are just as good as if you never had been bad." The Life-Principle, or God, never punishes and holds no grudges. When you forgive yourself, you are forgiven. Life forgives you when you forgive yourself and others. Your sense of guilt brought on the condition. Change your attitude now and you will cure the condition. Forgiveness is an exchange whereby you give up fear for faith in God, sickness for wholeness, poverty for wealth, and pain for peace. In other words, you give up negative and destructive emotions in exchange for harmony, health and peace of mind.

I gave her the following prayer to use frequently, making sure that she does not subsequently deny what she affirms: "All is Spirit and the manifestation of Spirit. My life is God's life; I am perfect now. All my organs are God's ideas, which minister and benefit me. I am a spiritual being: I am a perfect reflection of the Perfect God. I feel and know that I am perfect in all ways; I am spiritual, Divine and holy. I am one with my Father, and my Father is God. I am expressing harmony, peace and joy. All growth in my body and affairs is governed by Infinite Intelligence which is the active, all-wise, law-abiding Principle called God. I know that I am immersed in the Holy Omnipresence, and every atom, tissue, muscle and bone of my being is flooded with the radiance of the Light Limitless. My body is God's body; I am whole and perfect. I am one with God. My mind is flooded with the peace that passeth understanding, and all is well, I thank thee, Father."

I have heard from her recently, and she says that the edema has subsided, the calcareous deposits are disappearing and the pain is alleviated. As she continues, I know she will have a perfect healing.

In Zurich, the home of the late Carl Jung, there is a great spiritual awareness. Dr. Freitag frequently speaks to audiences in Switzerland and has a large following in several of the major cities. I experienced overflow audiences in all the cities visited, including Zurich.

In consultation with a woman in the hotel in Zurich, she said that she had given 100,000 francs to a con man. Apparently, she had experienced difficulty gaining admission to the United States, and he had told her he could fix it up for that sum of money. This was negligence, carelessness and indifference on her part. She had not consulted an attorney nor asked representatives in the office of the American Consulate about this proposed bribe. In other words, she did not use common sense.

She admitted that she had been foolish and gullible and a victim of a negative suggestion. Con men succeed many times in defrauding their victims because the victims don't reason things out and are greedy and looking for something for nothing. There is no free lunch. The suggestion of the con man that he could bribe an official and get her the visa and necessary papers triggered her false belief and ulterior motivation. Had she been honest, upright and on the level, the suggestion of bribing would have been rejected. It is rare that a con man can cheat an honest person. Remember that the suggestion of another has no power to create what he suggests. You can reject it. If accepted by you, then it becomes a movement of your own thought. The local authorities in Zurich informed this young woman that the same man had swindled many widows and was now in East Germany.

I suggested that she could not lose the money unless she admitted the loss mentally. I further suggested that she apply the following formula of prayer: "I am mentally and spiritually united with the 100,000 francs I gave to _____. It comes back to me multiplied in Divine order." I explained to her that she was not to subsequently deny what she affirmed and that her subconscious always magnifies what she contemplates. The return of the money will come to her in ways she knows not of. The ways of the subconscious are past finding out.

This took place about a month ago, and as of this writing I have not heard from her, but I know that as she remains faithful to her prayer, she will receive the answer, magnified and multiplied. Never admit a loss. You can always go back to the Center and claim your

good from the Infinite Storehouse within, and the
Spirit within will honor and validate your claim.

Why She Felt Guilty about Divorce

In the course of a conference with a woman in
Frankfurt, Germany, I learned that she felt guilty and
thought she had sinned grievously because she had
divorced her husband, who was an alcoholic and had
been very abusive to her and their two children. He
was also a non-provider.

I asked her if she didn't have a persistent feeling, an
inner intuitive perception, which lingered within her
prior to the marriage, and she said she did but did not
heed it. This was the inner voice of her Higher Self
seeking to protect her. It is that inner awareness, that
silent inner knowing, that always seeks to protect you.
There are many men and women who completely
reject these inner monitions, murmurings and whisperings of the heart strings. It is wrong to marry when
that inner knowing persists.

I explained to her that it is wrong to live a lie, and
that divorce was not wrong for her because both of
them were already divorced mentally from love, harmony, peace, honesty, integrity, kindness and goodwill.

She Quoted Matthew 19

Apparently she knew the verses by heart:
They say unto him, Why did Moses then command

*to give a writing of divorcement, and to put her
away?*

*He saith unto them, Moses because of the hardness
of your hearts suffered you to put away your wives:
but from the beginning it was not so.*

*And I say unto you, Whosoever shall put away his
wife, except it be for fornication, and shall marry
another, committeth adultery: and whoso marrieth
her which is put away doth commit adultery* (Matthew 19:7-9).

The Bible is a psychological and spiritual textbook
and must be interpreted from the standpoint of its
inner meaning. Ignorance of this inner meaning
causes endless confusion, guilt, misery and failure.
She had married outside the church and had had a
civil ceremony. Her relatives had told her that she had
sinned and inevitably would be punished.

The first thing you should learn about marriage is
that no rabbi, priest, minister or judge sanctifies a
marriage. All they do is to dramatize externally the
inner agreement between a man and a woman. Neither
does any church on the face of the earth sanctify a
marriage. Marriage is a union of two souls who sense
the Presence of God in each other. In other words,
each is united to the God-Presence within.

God Is Love

When two hearts unite in love and are honest, just
and sincere with each other, that is God, or pure love,
joining two people together. It is a union of two souls

seeking their way back to the heart of Reality. In a true sense, each is married or united to a God of love, for God is love.

I explained to her that marriage based on lies, falsehood or ulterior motivation is an absolute lie and completely false from all angles. It is foolish to say that God, or love, is present in all marriages. Her ex-husband had lied to her. He had never told her that he was an alcoholic, that he had been previously divorced three times and had abandoned his previous family. This so-called marriage was a complete farce, a sham and a masquerade. This woman realized that he had married her because she was wealthy, pretty and attractive and probably wanted to satisfy and compensate for his inferiority complex and failure in life.

Having explained the inner meaning of the verses she had referred to, there came to her a freedom from a sense of guilt based on early false indoctrination. I gave her the following prayer, telling her that she was not to deny what she affirmed. I explained that she does not get what she wants in life but that she gets according to the mental equivalent which must be established in her subconscious mind. In other words, as she thinks with interest on the qualities she admires in a man, she will gradually build up the ideal in her mind. Then, according to the law of the subconscious she will attract the embodiment of her ideal. This is the prayer I gave her:

"I know that I am one with God now. In Him I live, move and have my being. God is life; this life is the life of all men and women. We are all sons and daughters of the one Father.

"I know and believe there is a man waiting to love and cherish me. I know I can contribute to his happiness and peace. He loves my ideals, and I love his ideals. He does not want to make me over; neither do I want to make him over. There are mutual love, freedom and respect.

"There is one mind; I know him now in this mind. I unite now with the qualities and attributes that I admire and want expressed by my husband. I am one with them in my mind. We know and love each other already in Divine Mind. I see the God in him; he sees the God in me. Having met him *within,* I must meet him in the *without;* for this is the law of my own mind.

"These words go forth and accomplish whereunto they are sent. I know it is now done, finished and accomplished in God. Thank you, Father."

I have received a wonderful letter from this woman. She wrote that she is now happily married and is on a world tour. Love never faileth.

... What Therefore God Hath Joined Together, Let Not Man Put Asunder *(Matthew 19:6)*

The misinterpretation of this verse has brought about endless confusion plus a sense of guilt for a great number of people who think that because they were married in a particular church, divorce is wrong and sinful. Nothing could be further from the truth. God is love; and if love does not join two people together, there is no real marriage. God, or love, is not present in such unions; therefore, in reality, the whole performance is a sham.

As mentioned previously in earlier books, I perform marriage ceremonies for men and women here in Leisure World, some of whom are seventy-five and eighty years of age. Many times the man says that he is completely depleted sexually, but they are honest, just and perfectly frank with each other. Honesty, integrity, justice and goodwill are all children of love. Therefore, it is God, or love, joining the two together just as much as if they were twenty or twenty-one years of age.

The word *man*, as mentioned in the above Biblical verses, means manifestation on the objective screen of space. When love joins two together, no objective situation, condition, circumstance or inlaws can break it up. Nothing can oppose Divine love. All of us are living in a subjective and objective world, and we express objectively on the screen of space that which is impressed in our subconscious, or subjective mind. That is the meaning of the age-old Truth: "As within, so without."

Marriage Takes Place in the Mind

I have suggested to many women who know the laws of mind to select one person in the world who would love to hear good news about them, then, prior to sleep, to hear that person tell them over and over again what they long to hear. In that drowsy, sleepy state, there is an outcropping of your subconscious mind, and it is an excellent way to impregnate your deeper mind as you enter into the deep of sleep.

Many widows and others have said to me, "I have heard you say to me over and over again prior to sleep, 'I now pronounce you man and wife,' and I go off to the deep of sleep." The last waking concept is etched on your deeper mind. The wisdom of the subconscious decides how to bring it to pass. These women know that all transactions take place in the mind, and when they think of marriage they already know they will marry character, which is the ideal in mind. In prayer you always go to the end and, having seen and felt the end, you will experience the means to the realization of the end.

"I now pronounce you man and wife" are the words I would use at the end of the ceremony. Therefore, it has already happened in mind and must take place in the objective world. In nearly all instances the women who have used this technique have experienced the joy of the answered prayer. The outside ceremony, or marriage, confirmed the inside act of their imagination and feeling.

Ignorance Is the Only Sin and All the Suffering Is the Consequence

Buddha, in his meditation, asked the cause of all the suffering and misery in India. The answer he received was *ignorance*. Teach the people the Truth of Being. As you know, ignorance of the law is no excuse—this is true in civil cases. If you pass a red light, it is no use to plead ignorance of the civil code, or law. You are fined, nevertheless.

We Live Together; What Is the Difference?

I have heard that many times. The college boy who knows it all says, "I sleep with different girls and have sex with them. What's wrong with it?" I say to him, "What are you afraid of? Are you afraid to commit yourself? Are you shirking your responsibilities? Do you have an inferiority complex? Love is a state of at-one-ness. If you love a girl, you do not do anything unloving. You are dodging the issue. Love is always confirmed objectively. You must demonstrate your love."

I have talked with many young women who have lived with the "ideal boy." She loves him in her own way and wants him to marry her. She subconsciously forgets to take the pill and then becomes pregnant. Her story is very prevalent. He deserts her, claims he is not responsible, and claims it was someone else who got her pregnant. Where is the love? the honesty? the integrity?

"What nonsense," I say to these young men who tell me they sleep with many girls on the campus. "Why don't you invite your sister down to the campus and introduce her to all these wonderful lovers?"

The answer, of course, is, as you know very well, "Not my sister. I would kill her first." You see, it is always the other fellow's sister. What rank hypocrisy! When you hurt another, you are also hurting yourself.

Some of these girls who engage in what they call free love, when they become pregnant, feel full of guilt. Their so-called lovers usually desert them. Many times they commit suicide, or they become the ladies who walk the promiscuous path. The man who walks off and who is responsible also for their pregnancy and predicament cannot escape responsibility, and the law of his subconscious responds in its own way.

Take a good look at those people who say that they don't need a marriage ceremony or what they call a piece of paper. They are usually very insincere, full of fear, belligerent, bellicose and frightfully insecure. They are afraid that the union might not work. They are afraid of responsibility. There is no love there; therefore, the whole performance is rank hypocrisy.

Some will tell you that they are doing it, i.e., living together as man and wife, principally for tax purposes. That is completely false. I say to them, "All right. If you are married in your heart and it is true love, why don't you confirm it objectively? Everything that is subjectified is always made manifest in the objective world. If one of you died tonight, what provisions have you made to your partner? Supposing you passed on in your sleep tonight. Have you left an insurance policy of $100,000 or $200,000 for your spouse to take care of her or him? You must demonstrate your love."

I say to women: Pay no attention to what a man says. Watch what he does. What he does is what he means. Women, wake up!

Keep Thy Heart . . . for Out of It Are the Issues of Life *(Proverbs 4:23)*

The heart in Hebrew symbolism and in the figurative language of the Bible means your subconscious mind. This means that every action has an equal and corresponding reaction. It also means that whatever you convey with feeling to your subconscious will come forth as form, function, experience and event. Marriage is definitely of the heart (the seat of love) and not of the church, temple, magistrate or court. If that is true, which it is, there follows the outer to confirm the inner state of mind. Otherwise, there is something frightfully wrong. All actions of the union of the conscious and subconscious mind are confirmed in an objective fashion. The laws of mind proclaim that what you do within be experienced without.

What Is a True Marriage?

It is a marriage of the heart, and the heart, or subconscious mind, is the dwelling place of God. You are the temple of the Living God. All the powers of God are within you. You can call the power your Higher Self, I AM, Allah, Brahma, Ain Soph, the Oversoul or the Living Spirit Almighty. In reality, It has no name. The ancient mystics said: "When you name It, you cannot find It, and when you find It, you cannot name It."

A Visit to London

I established the Truth Forum in Caxton Hall, London, England, in the early fifties, which was conducted under the auspices of Dr. Evelyn Fleet. I have lectured there and given seminars over the years. On a recent trip, I had the privilege of ordaining Michael Grimes, who lectures on the laws of mind at Caxton Hall. He is a wonderful and outstanding teacher and a profound student of the Laws of Life and the way of the Holy Spirit.

On this recent visit to London, he graciously arranged a joint session of the Science of Mind and the Unity Movement in London, which is conducted by Dr. Ralph Seelig, who is also absolutely outstanding in his promotion of the great truths of life. He and his lovely wife are broadcasting the eternal verities in a wonderful way, and they are illumined and blessed in countless ways. Dr. Grimes and Dr. Seelig are doubly blessed by having the wonderful wives who urge them ever onward, upward and Godward.

MARRIAGE, SEX, AND DIVORCE

A Hopeless Marital Situation

A husband and wife visited me at the St. Ermin's Hotel next door to Caxton Hall, where I usually lecture when I visit London, England. They said they had been married in the Church of England but that their situation was intolerable. He admitted that he was cruel to her and had whipped her at times in order to get a sexual release, as he called it. The wife seemed to think that a divorce was a sin. She had weird, grotesque and superstitious beliefs of what marriage really meant.

I explained to them that marriage is not a license for cruelty, whipping, neglect and abuse. Her husband was obviously a psychopathic sadist. He admitted that he was a wife beater. Actually, his wife was his main support. Her clergyman had told her that she should stay with him regardless of his debaucheries and sexual abnormalities. This, of course, is absolutely stupid and makes no sense. There is no such teaching in any Bible of the world.

A great number of people, including some clergymen who should and would know better if they would study the exegesis of the Bible, or if they would read Philo Judaeus of 2000 years ago, who gave the allegorical exposition of the five Books of Moses, would then see that the whole Bible is allegorical, mystical, figurative, idiomatic, and full of fables, myths, cryptograms and numbers. The New Testament is full of parables, and nobody in his right mind takes all the parables literally.

For example, the words *fornication* and *adultery* in the Bible do not refer merely to the bodily acts. The mind acts upon the body. The body is a vehicle. It moves as it is moved upon. It acts as it is acted upon. The body does nothing unless it is acted upon by the mind. You can play on your body a melody of love or a hymn of hate. In other words, your body does nothing except on the orders of your mind. Surely that is simple and needs no explanation.

The Bible says, . . . *Whosoever looketh on a woman to lust after her hath committed adultery with her already in his heart* (Matthew 5:28). This reveals and portrays that adultery, first of all, is of the heart, or your subconscious mind. And, of course, your body is acted upon by what is impressed on your subconscious mind.

Your Body Is Not Responsible

The forces that govern your body are mental and spiritual. It is your mental attitude that determines your relationship with God, men and the universe. These two people saw the spiritual meaning of the Bible passages and, as a result, decided to dissolve the cruel hoax. They learned that fornication is actually idolatry, which means the worship of false gods, or cohabiting with evil in the bed of your mind.

266

If you give power to the stars, or if you say that others have power over you, or the fan gives you a stiff neck, etc., all of them are false gods in the sense that you are giving power to created things rather than to the Creator. You are fornicating, Biblically speaking, when you give power to voodooism, black magic, horoscopes, evil entities or any external power. God is the only Presence and Power. You cease fornicating when you give your supreme allegiance to the I AM within you, the only Presence and Power. When you cohabit with grudges, peeves, resentment and ill will in the bed of your mind, you will spawn an evil progeny.

The Bible is talking about the subjective side of life and does not refer to tenets, dogmas, formulations and prescribed rules for marriage established by various churches. Adultery and idolatry are the same thing. We speak of chemicals such as sodium chloride as C.P., meaning chemically pure. All adulterants are removed; no foreign substances are present. In a similar manner, you must cleanse your mind and cease giving power to externals, people, conditions and circumstances. In other words, cease worshipping false gods.

Spiritual-minded people do not give power to the phenomenalistic world. They give power to the Creator and not to the created thing. Adultery is of the heart (subconscious mind). The body does nothing of itself. Bodily actions are preceded by mental and emotional states. Whenever you mentally and emotionally unite with false ideas and superstitious concepts, you are fornicating. Whatever you mentally dwell upon and feel to be true impregnates your subconscious mind and is called a mental sex act. It is a union of your conscious and subconscious mind, and there is an offspring from that union, which is called the son, bearing witness of the father and mother. The son is the manifestation or objectification of your idea, whether good or bad.

Why She Nagged Him

A woman in London said that her husband had lost all his money in the stock market and that he felt morose, morbid and deeply depressed. He wanted a divorce, claiming that she was nagging him to death.

I explained to her that nagging was about the quickest way to dissolve a marriage and suggested to her that this is the time when he needs encouragement and support. She pointed out the good qualities and attitudes he had when she married him. I said to her that these same qualities and characteristics which endeared him to her in the first place are still there but need to be resurrected. This can be accomplished by scientific prayer.

I gave her the following prayer to use frequently, pointing out that he would subconsciously receive her spiritual upliftment and both would be blessed: "I know that my husband is receptive to my constructive thought and imagery. I claim, feel and know that at the center of his being is peace. My husband is Divinely guided in all ways. He is a channel for the Divine. God's love fills his mind and heart. There are harmony, peace, love and understanding between us. I picture him as happy, healthy, joyous, loving and prosperous. I surround and enfold him with the sacred circle of God's love which is impregnable, impervious and invulnerable to all negation."

They talked things over while I was in London and then decided to pray together and stay together. Her husband recently has found a very lucrative position. Prayer changes things: It changes the person who prays.

Keep your mind stayed on God and this will prevent your mind from wandering to the false gods and erroneous beliefs of the world. When difficulties arise in marriage relationships, the thing to do is to exalt God in each other. Talk to the Spirit of your wife or husband as follows: "The Spirit in me talks to the Spirit of John or Mary, and there are harmony, peace, love and understanding between us at all times. God thinks, speaks and acts through me, and God thinks, speaks and acts through my spouse." As you make a habit of this, the marriage will grow more blessed and beautiful through the years.

He Went Back to Her

A pharmacist in London had a quarrel with his wife. As a result, she left him and married someone else. He married someone else also. All the time, though, he was married in his heart to his first wife. She, too, longed for him and told him so. Love hath joined them in the first place. There was no real love in his present situation. He saw the point and let his heart's love unite them once more. It is wrong to live a lie. It is far more decent and honorable to break up the lie than live it.

The answer to every problem is spiritual awareness. To know how to pray scientifically would prevent many marriages from ever taking place. Likewise, when there is a spiritual awareness and a deep reverence for things Divine, many divorces would never take place. Only God and His love can bind up the wounds of the broken-hearted and set free the captives.

Disciplining the Mind

. . . *She was found with child of the Holy Ghost* (Matthew 1:18). The *Holy Ghost* means the Holy (whole) Spirit or God which is lodged in the unconscious depths of all men. *Joseph* is your choosing, volitional or conscious mind. *Mary* represents your deeper mind full of the qualities, attributes and potencies of God. Joseph, the conscious mind, should be a guide and protector for the holy child, which child is your awareness of the presence and power of God within you. Your thought is Joseph and your feeling or emotion is Mary. When these two unite in peace and harmony, your prayer is answered; this is God in action. This is the way your mind works, and the knowledge of this is the birth of the Holy Child or Wisdom in you.

Practice a harmonious, synchronous and joyous relationship between your conscious and subconscious mind, and you will bring forth health, peace, strength and security. Enthrone the right idea in your mind; then you will experience in your heart the true feeling. The union of your thought and feeling represents the married pair in you; when they are fused, the third element, peace (God), enters in and you experience the joy of the answered prayer. Let your heart become a chalice for God's love and a manger for His birth; then, as a result, you will express and bring forth a child which is God on earth.